RESIDENTIAL DESIGNS

RESIDENTIAL DESIGNS

How to Get the Most for Your Housing Dollar

Edited by David E. Link
Editor, *Professional Builder*

With Original Design Contributions by
Architect John D. Bloodgood, A.I.A.

CAHNERS BOOKS
Division of Cahners Publishing Company, Inc.
89 Franklin Street, Boston, Massachusetts 02110

Library of Congress Catalog Card Number: 73-76442
International Standard Book Number: 0-8436-0116-7
New material copyright © 1974 by Cahners Publishing Company, Inc.
Copyright 1967, 1968, 1969, 1970, 1971, 1972 by *Professional Builder,*
A Cahners Publication
Printed in the United States of America
Halliday Lithograph Corporation, West Hanover, Massachusetts

Contents

Preface   vii

Acknowledgments   ix

1 CREATING THE TOTAL ENVIRONMENT   1
How to create the total housing package that
today's buyers demand

2 CAPITALIZE ON THE SITE   9
A good subdivision plan eliminates the line-up
look and divides lots into a variety of shapes

3 ELEVATIONS, PROPORTION, SCALE AND TEXTURE   17
How to design a better exterior for the
one-story, two-story and split-level house

4 THE LOW COST EXTERIOR   25
Build in visual interest on a modest budget

5 THE THIRD DIMENSION   33
How to put all three spatial dimensions
to work

6 DESIGNING THE MANUFACTURED HOUSE   41
How the modular puzzles can be made to
fit the buyer's demands

7 APARTMENT PLANNING   53
Cut waste; dramatize apartment living

8 OUTDOOR LIVING   65
Create visual impact and livability by tying
the indoors to the outdoors

9 EXTERIOR HANDLING OF DOORS AND WINDOWS   75
Easy paths to variety and style in
exterior designs

10 INTERIOR HANDLING OF DOORS AND WINDOWS   85
How to add character to large and
small rooms

11 KITCHENS   **97**
In low cost, medium priced or luxury housing,
kitchens can provide buyer appeal

12 KITCHEN REMODELING   **109**
Builder recipes for stretching space
and storage

13 SECOND BATH NEED NOT BE SECOND BEST   **121**
Ideas on how to help the second or
third bathroom ''work harder''

14 STORAGE: HOUSING FOR POSSESSIONS   **128**
Get maximum utility and sales value
for every square foot

15 STRUCTURAL LIGHTING   **141**
Built-in lighting can stretch space,
dramatize height and create a buying mood

16 CUSTOM CONCEPTS   **152**
How to give a tailored look to
merchant built housing

Preface

At a time when American households are demanding better housing in a better environment, yet at a price they can afford, the need for good design and land planning in residential construction has never been more critical. The collection of ideas illustrated and discussed in this book are dedicated to the continuing improvement of our residential environment, both inside the dwelling itself and within the total community.

What's needed is a continual upgrading in both quality and techniques in residential design. Involved are the elements of good floor plans, exciting interior and exterior design, practical handling of space for the automobile, and the clustering of houses, townhouses, and apartments to conserve on land costs and to provide necessary open spaces.

No one book can contain all of the ideas for good execution of all of these elements, and this book makes no such claim.

The chapters in this collection were originally published as part of "Design Lab," a continuing series in *Professional Builder* Magazine, a business publication for the housing and light construction industry. The objective was to help the builder/developer bring new thinking to bear on his role in providing shelter and creating an environment that would add to the marketability and value of his product.

In trying to meet this objective, the effort was to isolate each phase of residential planning for purposes of discussion. Yet there was a continual realization that each element of design is inextricably related to all other elements in the overall plan; for example, elevations and window placements are affected by siting as are floor plans, size, patios, decks, etc.

Since this series deals with fundamentals, it was logical to start with the most basic factor affecting the design of a home — the land itself. Thus, the early chapters deal with the problems of creating the total environment and with siting the individual lot within the total development.

As the reader goes through the book, it will be obvious that the original audience was the builder/developer. However, the ideas and the specific drawings should also hold particular interest for architectural students, investors and lenders in real estate, and those individuals thinking of buying or building a house.

In publishing this collection in book form, it is hoped that the ideas in it can help all of those involved in the process of residential planning and design — from the builder, lender, politician, to the ultimate consumer — do a better job in improving our residential environment.

Acknowledgments

Many persons helped contribute to this collection of residential design ideas. These include the key editors of *Professional Builder* Magazine, its various art directors, and its architectural illustrator, Roger Jadown.

The major effort in creativity, however, comes from John D. Bloodgood, the magazine's design consultant and a nationally recognized architect. A member of the American Institute of Architects, Mr. Bloodgood is headquartered in Des Moines, Iowa. He has worked with large and small builders of housing throughout the country. His designs for individual houses and for communities have won many awards. Without the many hours of creative thought from him, this book would not have been possible.

1
Creating the Total Environment

The word "environment" is very popular today. It is on the
lips of politicians, educators, architects, journalists, and more to
the point — the consumer. Everyone is concerned with the way in
which people relate to the land. The consumers are more aware of
ugliness, of blight, of urban decay, suburban sprawl. They have
been told that the housing industry has failed to contribute
solutions to our environmental problems; that it has created
communities that lack variety, or otherwise fail to meet the full
human needs of their inhabitants. But the housing industry is —
and has been for some time — trying, in the face of some great
difficulties and often with little help, to remedy the situation.
Builders like James Rouse of Columbia, Md., the Paparazzo
Brothers in New York, Emil Hanslin in Mass., the Irvine Company
in Calif., Vernon Young in Houston, Bruce Bleitz in Chicago,
Fred Kemp in St. Louis, just to name a few, have grappled with
the problem of creating more than mere shelter. They have created
pleasant communities that recognize the recreational, social and
aesthetic needs of the people who will live in them. And they have
been successful in selling their ideas to a very receptive public.

Creating the total environment is not a mysterious art; no
wizardry is necessary. All that is needed is the most logical
application of the principles that relate people to the
space around them.

Total Environment Begins with a Single Lot

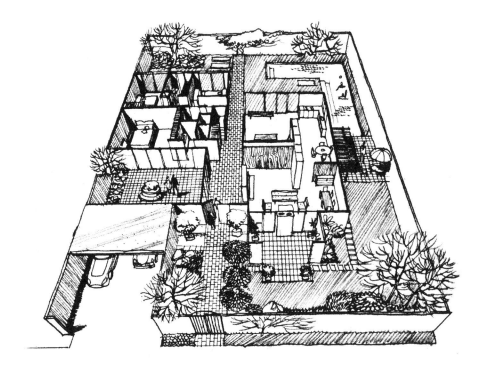

Total environment implies the intelligent planning of space as it relates to its use by people. It does not only mean a grand plan involving thousands of units. In fact it begins with the logical division of spaces on a single lot. The example above is taken from Casas Capistrano near Los Angeles.

Every inch of the lot is used to best advantage. By placing the house off-center, useless sideyards are eliminated and a small but pleasant space is created for outdoor dining. The L-shape pool also utilizes the space created by this off-center treatment. The front of the lot is used for parking, entry court, and an outdoor "conversation area." Maximum privacy is obtained by placing the major living areas in the rear of the house, bedrooms are carefully zoned away from the active zone, and the master suite has its own private patio.

Spaces relate to one another in a logical fashion. Where a blend of indoor and outdoor living is desirable, it is provided; where privacy is a dominant need, or a feeling of intimacy is of a prime importance, areas are enclosed.

After solving the problem of the individual lot, attention must be focused on the street, or neighborhood. Builders and land planners have learned to mix housing styles, and housing types. Single family detached units mix happily with townhouses and small apartment buildings. In a community of all detached housing, clusters improve siting.

But everyone is in agreement that more must be done in the following areas:

1. Parking must be made more unobtrusive.
2. Pedestrian and vehicular traffic must be separated.
3. The character of the land must be preserved as much as possible.
4. Plantings and street furniture, including sign control, must be improved.

In the sketch below, garages and/or carports take care of parking for the single family home in the conventional manner. But in the townhouses, the planners have placed parking in the rear. Pedestrian traffic need not follow the contours of the street. In fact, sidewalks should follow natural pedestrian patterns like paths. Where they intersect the access or collector streets, a small underpass keeps people and traffic separate.

Planters, benches, street lighting, traffic signs, are all designed to give the community character and eliminate the jumble of hardware that so often ruins an otherwise pleasant neighborhood. Where density makes it economically feasible, extras such as a fountain can do much to create a focal point in what might be a dead, uninteresting space.

Everybody's Needs Must Be Met

The design and execution of entire communities has become increasingly important. The population explosion, along with the increasing scarcity of urban and suburban land, has forced developers to think of whole communities or new towns as the next step in solving the nation's housing needs.

In these new communities the task of creating total environment reaches its largest proportions. In smaller communities which are near a city or established town, the new community can borrow some of the existing facilities of its older neighbors. But in these new communities, all the needs of the future inhabitants must be met. Aside from providing basic housing types for a variety of family structures and incomes, provisions must be made for . . . recreational, social, commercial, and even industrial facilities.

The plan on this page is an excellent example of a new community. Recreational facilities surround and cut into it. Beaches, marinas, golf courses, club houses, meeting rooms are all provided to take care of the social and recreational requirements. A shopping center and office building not only provide the residents with needed retail outlets and space for professional offices, but they also become an important part of their social lives. Today's shopping center is often (if well planned) used by the community for summer concerts and art shows.

Green spaces are possible due to cluster planning and townhouse grouping. Pedestrian walkways keep children out of the way of cars. Feeder and collector streets are never zipped through the center, but curved so that traffic is automatically controlled. Intersections are kept to a minimum or eliminated entirely.

In the sketch on this spread there are four housing types: the townhouses, medium-rise, single family detached and high-rise. Their styles, while different, are compatible.

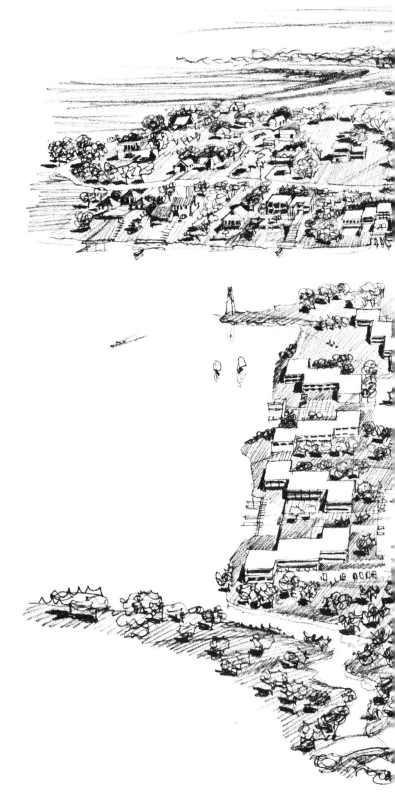

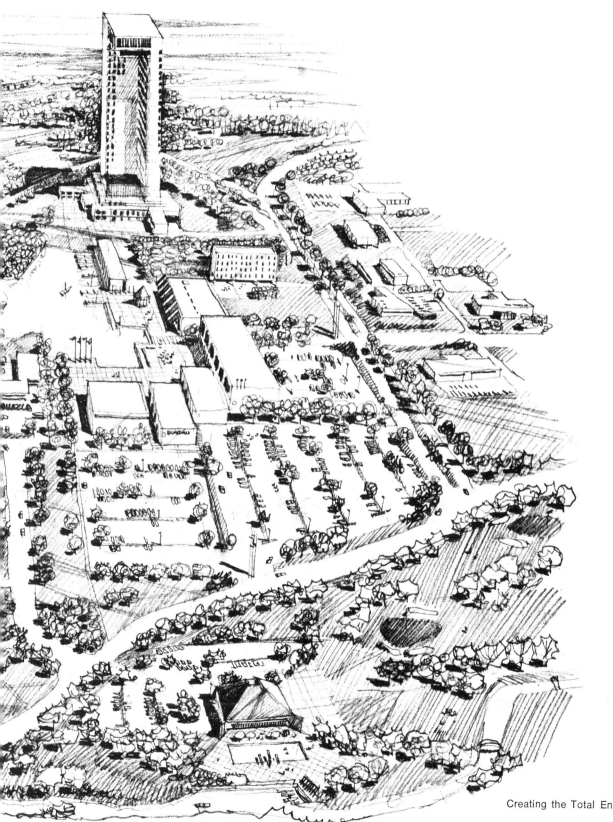

The Automobile Need Not Be an Intruder

Famous architects and planners such as John Cordwell who has designed Sandburg Village in Chicago, and numerous smaller suburban projects claim that "parking and the movement of traffic are the most serious problems affecting the success or failure of a community."

Lawrence Halprin, landscape architect and land planner in San Francisco, also feels this way.

In high density urban communities, such as the one pictured at right, the automobile has for some time reigned almost supreme. There isn't enough space to separate cars from people in the same manner that might be used in a new planned-unit-development. The answer to this problem often lies in a multi-level approach. In this illustration pedestrians are moved above the traffic. Overpasses take them over streets into pedestrian shopping malls. Cars move — and are parked — below the mall level. The interior courts created by the buildings shield the eye from traffic passing on the perimeter of the development.

Old streets that once bisected the residential part of the plan have been closed. Traffic is now routed around them, and the spaces created have been transformed into pleasant malls.

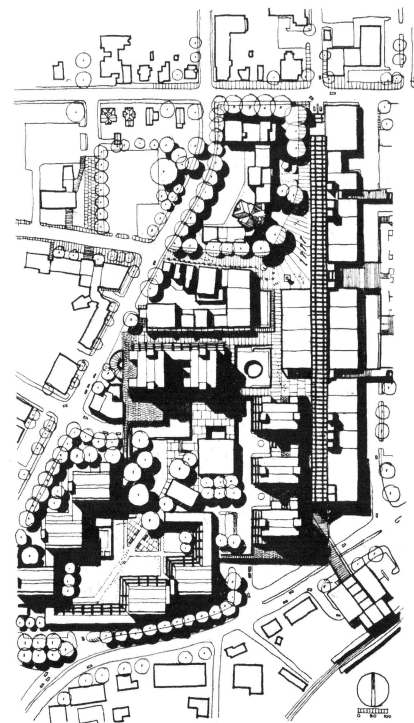

The success of the four solutions to parking shown here depends upon their locations in the overall plan. There are two simple general rules: keep them as small as possible (two smaller lots are easier to obscure than one large one) and place them where they will be convenient but not a dominant factor in the lives of the residents. The first illustration shows how some earthmoving can reap great some earthmoving can reap great dividends. Mounds of earth five feet high and properly planted can cut the viewline and greatly improve the appearance of a group of townhouses. Planners tend to forget that the average height of a man is 5'10". But keep in mind there are many ways to break the view. Where possible, brick or stone walls are desirable. They also shield the cars from view with the added advantage of introducing texture and architecture to the landscape.

The last solution to the parking problem is the best, but the most expensive. Underground parking totally eliminates the lot, freeing more land for recreation or park.

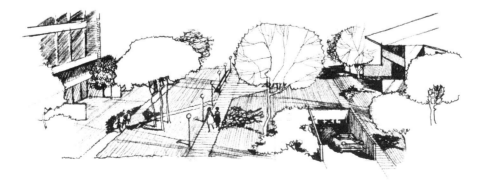

Spatial Contrasts Relieve the High Density Look

There need not be a crowded or confined feeling to a high density development. The proper balance of large and small spaces will relieve the monotony that ruins so many conventionally planned communities.

Small patches of common lawn, or walkways that open out onto a larger space (such as a green belt or recreational area) provide the eye with a variety of short, medium and long-range views. More space should be provided around larger masses such as a high rise apartment building; less around clusters of homes or garden apartments.

By mixing not only housing types, but also the spatial relationships between them, planners achieve both high density and livability.

2
Capitalize on the Site

The most basic factor affecting the design of any residence is the land itself. The individual building site — its shape, size and contour — should be planned so that maximum use is made of the land's natural assets. At the same time, the plan should be such that it guarantees each home owner within the development full use of his individual lot.

This chapter offers suggestions for orientation of the house on its individual site to take the best advantage of the natural terrain and sunshine. And it seeks to provide solutions for adding privacy for individual houses that are located within relatively dense subdivisions.

Privacy and Utility, Not Streetscapes

A good plan eliminates the line-up look, divides lots into a variety of shapes and sizes. The results are two-fold: first, the land plan itself is more interesting. The curved street is not only pleasant to look at, but also slows traffic. The second benefit lies in the opportunities for siting created by the variety of lots. Some lots are wide, some narrow, some pie-shaped, some inverted, some square. The challenge is to site each home on its lot in the most rational and meaningful way.

Once land was divided with a ruler. Houses were lined up like so many tin soldiers — all in neat rows facing one another.

But today, our concern with providing something better has forced us to think of different ways of structuring a community. We think in terms of cluster planning, traffic control, cul-de-sacs, curvilinear streets, open spaces, green belts, etc.

Examine the plan below. There are many siting principles working at the same time. The most important are:

1. Most houses avoid a western exposure.
2. A great degree of privacy is created for each family. The arrows illustrate the direction of the major glass areas.
3. Housing styles are automatically mixed because of the different demands of each lot.
4. Rooflines — flat and pitched — alternate or change direction to break up the "level" look that ruins so many communities.
5. Most importantly, each house *uses* its lot. Small, narrow lots tend to be surrounded by the house. By putting the garage in front, and setting the house on the back of the lot, an interesting, private outdoor living space is created in the center. Wider, square or rectangular lots are given an atrium L-shaped treatment. Triangular lots are treated in two ways. One plan reverses the house, places it on the front of the lot with the living space and major glass areas facing the rear; the other places the house to one side of the lot so that major glass areas and outdoor living space overlook its widest portion.

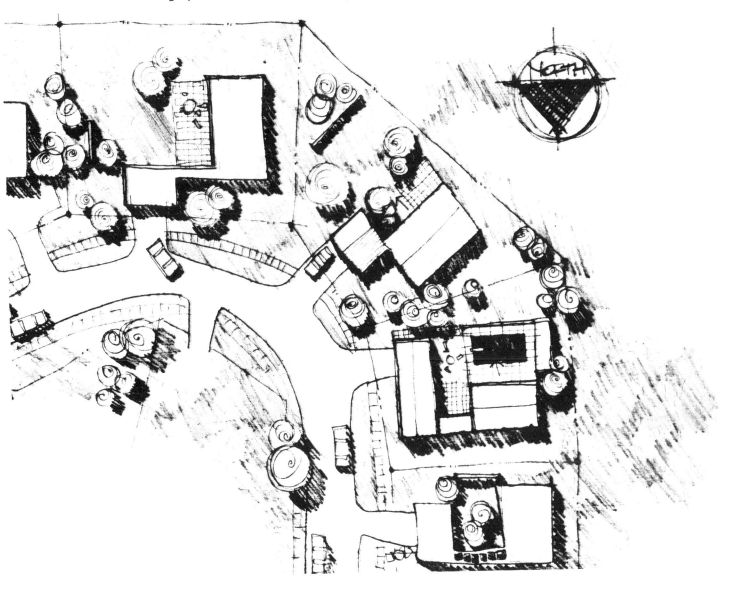

Relating the House to the Site

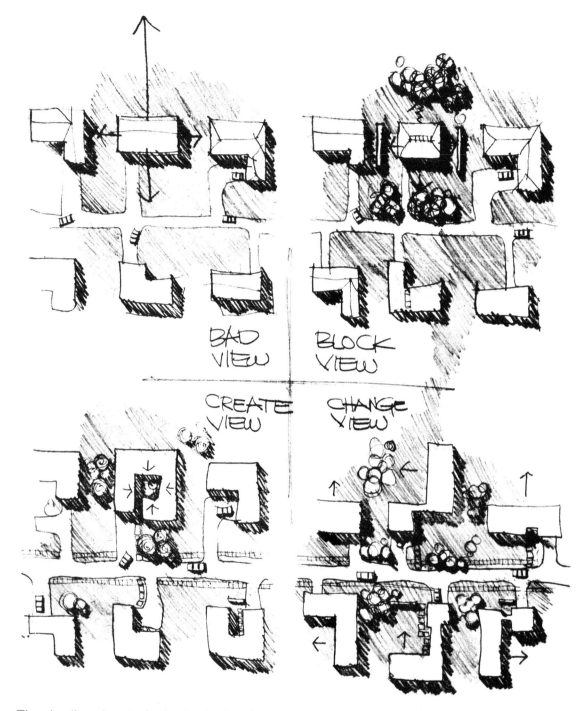

BAD VIEW

BLOCK VIEW

CREATE VIEW

CHANGE VIEW

The viewlines in a typical suburb often fail to be meaningful. The sketches illustrated on these pages show us some of the ways to improve the viewlines by siting or planting.

The series of sketches above show the viewline in three approaches to improve siting. The first, block view, is the simplest and is accomplished with strategically placed landscaping.

There are also ways to improve each home's siting by changing just a few of the houses in an area. Through the introduction of an atrium and a courtyard home — interspersed with more conventional homes — a great degree of privacy and variety is achieved. The atrium turns "viewlines" inside out. This immediately affects the adjoining houses, enabling them to be oriented to the side of their lots.

The last example demonstrates how views can be totally changed by alternating major glass

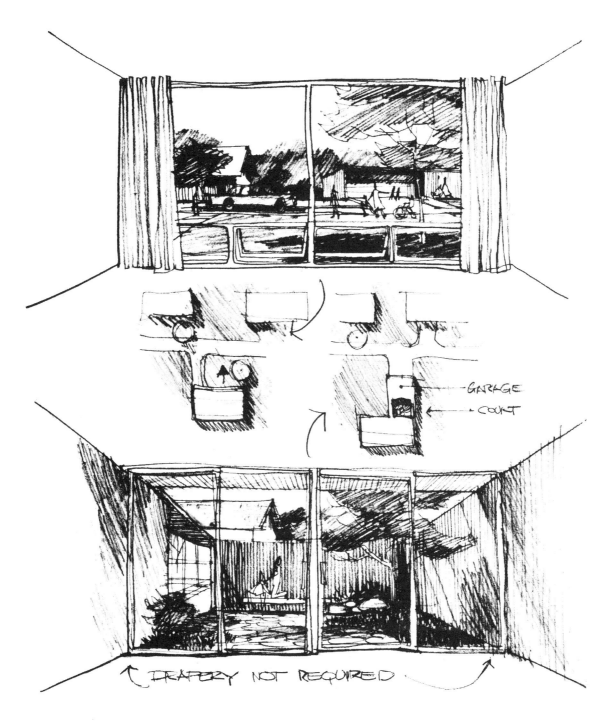

GARAGE
COURT

DRAPERY NOT REQUIRED

expanses so that some homes have them in the rear, others either to the left or to the right. Along with proper planting each home views its own lot, never its neighbor's.

The illustration above dramatizes the effect good siting or block-view planning has on a home's interior. The living room which overlooks the front lawn, curb, parked cars and house across the street, ends at the window. But the house with the block view (created in this case by placing the garage in front and fencing the sides) seems far larger. The living room not only looks larger, but actually is, since much of the land previously wasted on streetscape, has been incorporated into the private living space of the home.

Grade Determines Housing Types

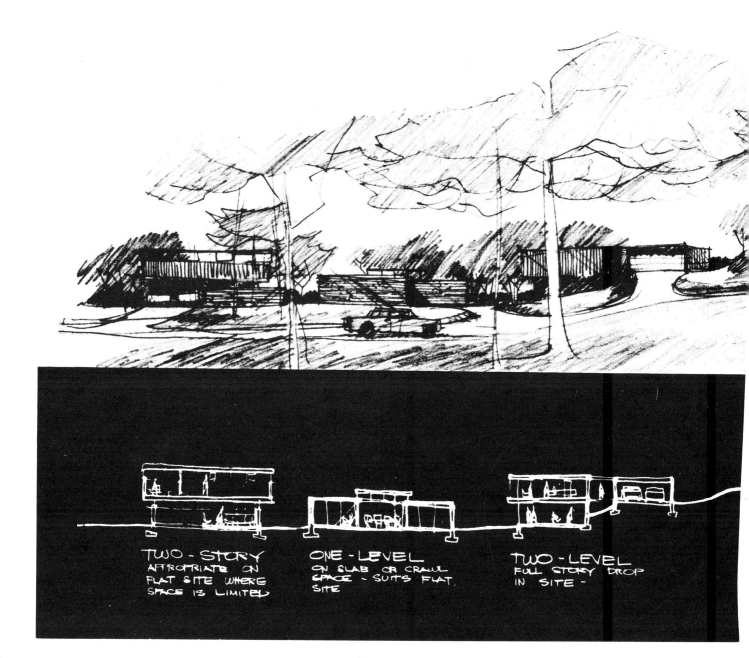

TWO - STORY
APPROPRIATE ON
FLAT SITE WHERE
SPACE IS LIMITED

ONE - LEVEL
ON SLAB OR CRAWL
SPACE - SUITS FLAT.
SITE

TWO - LEVEL
FULL STORY DROP
IN SITE -

The shape and size of a lot takes into account only two dimensions. There is a third: grade. The land's natural contour should be kept intact as much as possible. And the house should be an appropriate solution to the problems it poses. The illustration below gives you a cross-section of types of contours, and the houses which most appropriately belong.

Many times tri-levels look uncomfortable on an almost level piece of land — as if the house were trying to "sit down" and couldn't make it.

Land contour, along with lot size and shape, should determine the basic type of house. Obviously a small, narrow lot, such as some of the ones on the preceding page, force the builder to be more economical and plan a two or three level home. But the contour of the small lot will determine whether it should be a tri-level, mid-entry, two-story, or multi-level home.

This sketch illustrates both how a house fits into its lot, and how the resulting variety of levels affects the aesthetics of the community.

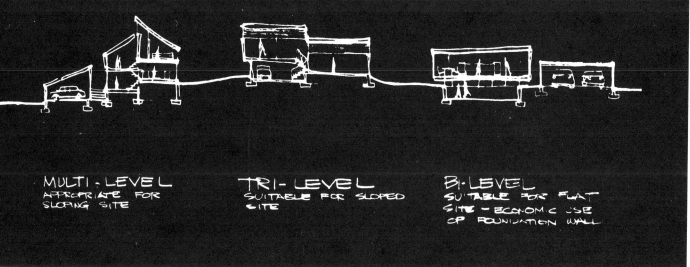

MULTI-LEVEL
APPROPRIATE FOR
SLOPING SITE

TRI-LEVEL
SUITABLE FOR SLOPED
SITE

BI-LEVEL
SUITABLE FOR FLAT
SITE — ECONOMIC USE
OF FOUNDATION WALL

Basic Astronomy Can Improve Livability

When a home has a southerly exposure, a little basic astronomy can contribute to a home's livability.

Since the sun's angle changes from season to season — lower on the horizon in the winter and higher in the summer — the addition of a four foot overhang can shield a major glass area from the relentless heat of the summer's sun, and also allow the lower winter sun to help warm the home.

This point is particularly important today since so many homes (traditional as well as contemporary) have large expanses of glass.

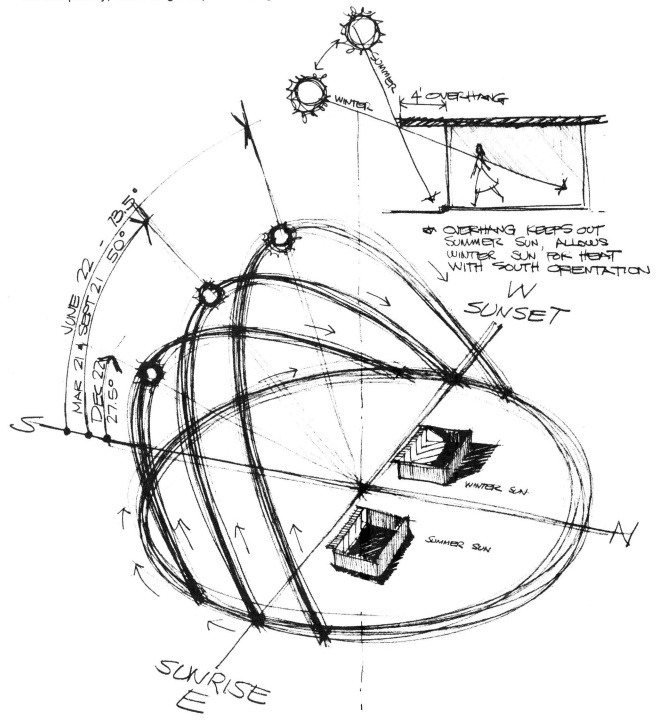

3 Elevations, Proportion, Scale and Texture

Elevation must never be confused with "facade." It is not something that is slapped onto the front of a house to dress it up. It is not a slipcover hiding worn out ideas. If thought of this way, an elevation will not relate to the house, it will fail. Successful elevations — whatever their style — all have one thing in common: they are logical, controlled extensions of the total plan of the house.

Many of the decisions regarding elevations are predicated on solutions to the earlier problems of size, floor plan, numbers of levels, etc. In turn, many of these decisions stem from given conditions: lot size, contour, natural amenities, view and exposure. It is pointless to force an elevation on a house that fights it. Allow the house and the site itself to "suggest" an elevation, then choose a style, and proceed with the final planning.

This chapter is specifically concerned with this final planning. There are rules which make a merely adequate design a good one. They involve selection of details, good proportion, and scale. Rules of proportion relate each element to the house as a whole: scale relates the elements to man. The proper selection of details — finishing materials, window and door styles, hardware — can give a house a unified design rather than a hodge-podge of styles and ornament.

To more clearly illustrate how these rules work, housing types — one story, two story, split level — are grouped together. This should serve to emphasize that it is the type and size of the house, not the style alone, that will most influence elevation. Within each grouping, various sizes and shapes in both traditional and contemporary styles are included.

The One Story House — Solutions to Size and Shape

The L-shape house presents a perfect opportunity to create an interesting and inviting enclosure at the entrance. With the help of plantings at the open end of the L, an intimate and private effect is created with a small space. The ends of the L form two masses which must be unified. Repetition of materials, perhaps a unifying planter, will keep the house from being split into two designs. If the garage is at one end of the L, as it is here, paint the door the same color and hue as the brick or siding.

The small house needs material organization, and line to accent length. The secret is that four elements (two windows, door, garage door) are held together by even spacing and common material between them. Thus, four elements become one mass, freeing a significant space for unbroken masonry treatment. This adds to the illusion of size. The line of overhang, broken once to avoid boxiness, adds length.

The U-shape house is particularly desirable on a city lot where privacy is difficult to achieve. The atrium court that is formed produces an "other-wordly" effect at the entrance, and also allows major glass areas to face a private garden rather than the street. A problem that often arises with a U-shape house is the blind-front look. This can be overcome by using an interesting pattern in the front walls and an importantly treated entry. A flat roof is always helpful in an atrium or U-shape house because it keeps the opening as light and airy as possible. It also eliminates another large blank mass on top of the windowless front elevation.

The long house (left) presents an opportunity to add an interesting variety of planes to the front of the house. The roof line must be broken to avoid monotony. Here one bedroom sash and entry are combined and projected two feet forward. The garage is also treated as a separate entity and it is recessed two feet. The resulting roof line tends to draw the eye from the ends of the house to its center. Some variety of sash adds interest to a long house, but one change is probably enough.

The flat ranch, so often an uninteresting string of windows and doors, can be given dimension and focus by extending a portion of the roof over the front entry. Three things happen: a broken horizontal line adds interest to the roof, shadow patterns create a feeling of depth, and the entrance is given importance. Remember to keep the additional elements in scale. Large pillars would be inappropriate, but informal rough-hewn planks are the right size — not too massive and not too delicate.

The Two Story House —
Need for Attention to Detail

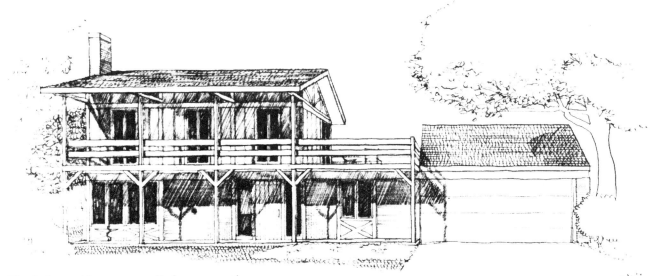

The informal house usually has several types of offsets and siding projections, but be careful not to overdo it. Porches and overhangs give interesting shadow patterns, but too many angles can create confusion. Sashes can be grouped. Balance comes from materials and color as much as from any regularity of window placement. Scale is a little freer. Trim and railings, decoration, etc. can be larger and more rough-hewn.

A contemporary effect is often difficult to achieve with a two story house. Here the mansard "hat" creates the story-and-a-half look and brings the house's silhouette closer to the ground. Proportion and scale alone act as ornamentation. Materials are natural and relate to the site. Various elements should be used in neat groupings. For most residential situations, it is better to strive for a simple straight-forward design, rather than something self-consciously "modern."

The traditional house should not be tampered with. The authentic look is achieved only by careful attention to detail: use narrow siding (4, 6, or maximum of 8 in.) on all sides of the house. Use double hung sash windows but never butt two together. Single windows help maintain proper vertical proportion. Corners gain design clarity with corner boards. Always use them to cover front and ends of applied masonry facing. Choose hardware and mouldings that are appropriate to the specific period not just something that looks "traditional."

The formal house (bottom) achieves its imposing appearance as a result of careful interplay of proportionate masses. The roof pitch should be a minimum of 6/12. Overhangs, projections, and applied ornamentation are generally absent. Decorative value comes from mouldings and shutters. A front paved platform or brick wall is often necessary to give it a setting and tie it to the ground. In formal designs the sashes are always repeated in balanced patterns.

The Split Level — Challenge to Make Sense

The multi-level split is the most direct and honest approach. It unabashedly follows the contour of the land. Floor levels describe themselves in relation to the slope. Each level becomes an individual unit. The grouping of these units becomes the ornamentation itself, so no other decoration is necessary.

Side-to-side split houses need to have a break in the facade plane where the break of level occurs. Here bedroom wing overhang makes the proportion of this wing seem proper. Garage is covered with board and batt plywood to match bedroom section tying whole house together: To achieve "country" look, all trim members should be rather heavy in scale, and rough textured. But remember, larger elements mean fewer elements.

THE LONG RANCH

The split entry house has an unusual proportion, grade-to-roof. In order to relate it to site, and give entrance doors relation to fenestration and a human scale, some other ground level element should be attempted. Here, the garage is also at grade and tied to entrance with a common porch. Large living room sash at top left balances garage wing. Note that siding is carried all the way down to grade.

A contemporary split ties itself to grade by a front porch projecting over a 2 ft. house extension. The roof is projected 4 ft., thus lowering the horizontal line. Large chimney mass further ties the house to site. Entrance area is given importance with a large fixed glass area which also allows entry to be at the side of the split entry platform. Notice that batten relates to grade rather than floor structure. This also helps give proper scale to the house.

4
The Low Cost Exterior

Despite trends toward clustering and use of townhouse or rowhouse design to achieve the most efficient plan for shelter, the market for the low cost detached single family house continues to hold significant demand. Here, and on the following pages in this chapter are design solutions that can add architectural interest to the five basic plans that are most often used in the low cost single family detached house.

Break the monotony of box in a long ranch

The ranch house, sited long axis parallel to the street, gains benefit from line and roof extensions to break the box shape, add shadow pattern and a feeling of depth. Two front bedroom closets (left) are extended to create forward-thrusting design element. Roof is extended from closet to wing wall just beyond entry to provide shadow, feeling of shelter. Brick veneer is held to massive block in center section, making it important and natural. Garage wall is extended to the rear to form fence for play yard-patio; it also gives ground-hugging feeling, relieving the boxy shape.

THE SPLIT ENTRY

THE 1½ STORY

Split entry gains character with ground-level detail

Often sited on flat land, the split entry design presents difficult height-vs.-width visual effect. Design gains character by pushing garage mass forward, as shown in sketch. This creates break from the box, adds to feeling of width, provides definition for entry court. Projections at bedroom sash (left side) give unified look to various window sizes, helps focus main attention on entrance door at mid-level. Steep roof pitch ($^9/_{12}$) gives more important look to house. Trim and detail is carried around all four sides for the "completed" look.

Ground-hugging treatment for 1½ - story house

It is important to site the story-and-a-half house as low to ground as possible and to extend as many horizontal lines as possible. Sketch shows how garage roof is continuation of main roof area, with forward projection relating to lower garage floor. Result is a relief from pinched top look of too steep a roof. Roof is extended further across living room sash and front door to create feeling of shelter, shadow. Garage door is surfaced with plywood siding to match house siding. Windows are grouped for simplicity, interest and stronger horizontal feeling.

The Low-cost Exterior

END TO THE STREET

Narrow house requires facade importance

Ranch, sited end to the street, calls for designing as much importance as possible into the usual 24-ft. width. Objective is to create suggestion of greater scale of depth. One technique is to use a side roof extension, even if it is just open to the rafters, for either a carport or entrance walk. This gives house some balance and interest, eases the usual "blank" look. Entrance is given as much importance as possible. This can be done with side wing wall effect (as shown), or via dominant traditional door surround or canopy. The roof pitch can be increased to add to the visual massing. A $5/12$ or $6/12$ pitch is much better than a $3/12$ pitch for a 24-ft width. Generous roof overhang should be used, especially at front.

ZERO LOT LINE

Blend garage, house in zero lot line design

The zero lot line house, if it has a garage, is usually dominated in width by the 18-ft. overhead door and driveway. It is most important to make the garage seem more like part of the house, and to suggest the invitation to walk back into the house itself. In this sketch, the garage dominance is given more importance and recognition with a staunch-looking wall projection. Door is covered with plywood to make it warmer, more residential in character. Lower front court wall extends forward of garage face to focus interest within the court. Roof lines are treated with strong horizontal emphasis. With close neighbors, each house is given individual look with door treatment, court walls.

The Third Dimension

How to Provide Design Excitement With Three-Dimensional Space Planning

Narrow Townhouse

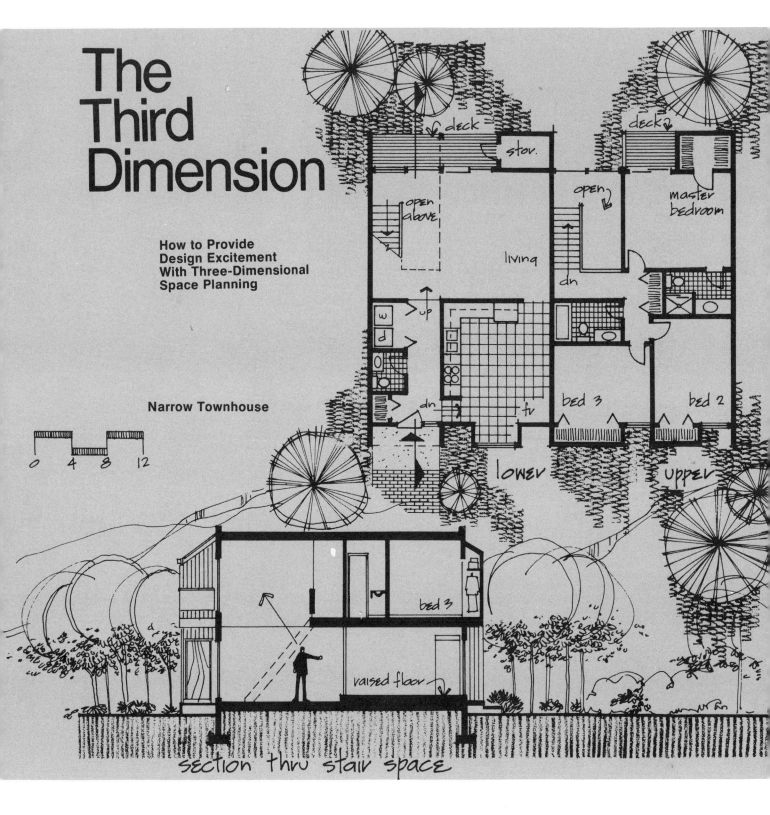

0 4 8 12

deck

stov.

open above

living

up

dn

lower

open

dn

master bedroom

bed 3

bed 2

upper

deck 2

fv

bed 3

raised floor

section thru stair space

5
The Third Dimension

The third dimension is the element that provides spatial excitement to any living space. It's the element that brings depth and visual interest into a room. And since it's already there, the smart designer and builder simply finds a way to capitalize on that third dimension. Use of the third dimension is often the least costly and most feasible method of space expansion.

In narrow townhouses, for example, there is danger of creating a funneled-railroad-car feeling of space. Utilization of vertical space can help avoid this, as suggested in the plan and elevation drawing at left.

The open stairwell and balcony give the living area a spacious excitement and luxury feeling despite its basic 20' x 28' floor dimension.

Three dimensional scale and appeal can be carried to the exterior, too. In the example illustrated, the glass wall at the first floor deck is continued to the master bedroom and balcony. Rear elevation incorporates a wing wall and storage unit to relieve the usual row house dullness.

The 1-1/2-Story Single Family

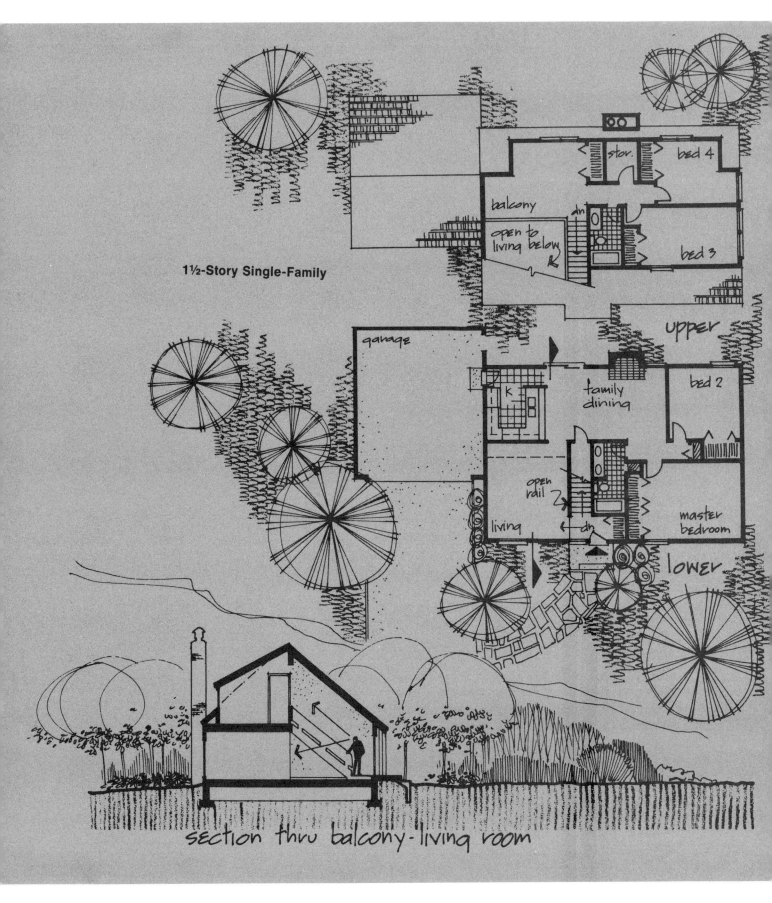

1½-Story Single-Family

balcony

open to living below

stor.

bed 4

dn

bed 3

upper

garage

k

family dining

bed 2

open rail

living

dn

master bedroom

lower

section thru balcony · living room

In the story and a half house, ordinary space can be turned into visual excitement by using the natural attributes of a steep roof pitch. The resulting balcony, (left), provides both sales appeal and functional space. Bedrooms three and four can be left closed off and optionally unfinished to keep initial costs down.

The entrance platform gives extra dimensional scale to the open vertical space. For maximum effect, this platform (on 2 x 6 sleepers over main floor construction) should be floored in a similar color but different material as the living room carpeting.

The floor plan shows how maximum through-house views can be used to minimize small boxy room feelings. Here, sliding glass door in the family room is placed so that when a visitor steps from entrance into living room he can see through to the outdoor patio. And in the family area, the kitchen has only a 43-inch high divider to block view of counter clutter but not the added visual continuity of both rooms.

The Split Entry

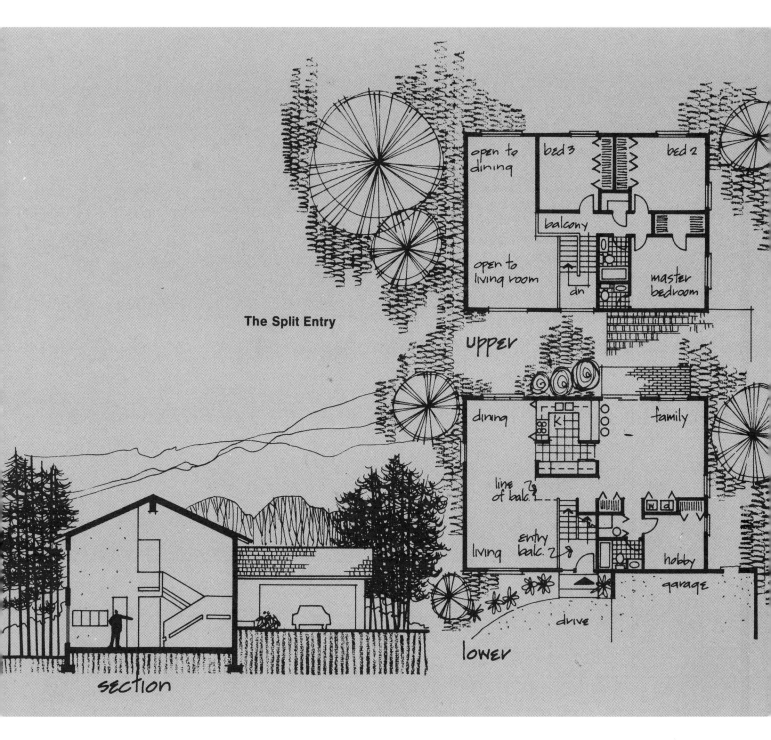

open to dining   bed 3   bed 2

balcony

open to living room   dn   master bedroom

The Split Entry

upper

dining   K   family

line of balc.

living   entry balc. 2   hobby   garage

drive

lower

section

The split-entry house can take on a strong custom design appearance when three-dimensional space planning is used to its fullest. Sketch and floor plan (left) show how the usual mid-level entrance can be changed from a caged-like feeling to one of space-expanding entrance balcony. Lower-level living room has a full two-story high ceiling, with a resulting dramatic spatial effect.

The upper-level plan allows more spacious bedrooms than can be achieved in the usual split-entry small-perimeter house. Crammed rooms on upper level of typical plan are exchanged for the open feeling of balconies, vaulted ceilings and minimal hall space.

Three-dimensional space planning can give impact to small spaces as well. Note here how the walk-in feature has been used in both linen closet and master bedroom closet. An extra foot or so of depth in a closet can change a flat-looking necessity into a three-dimensional selling feature.

The Zero Lot Line

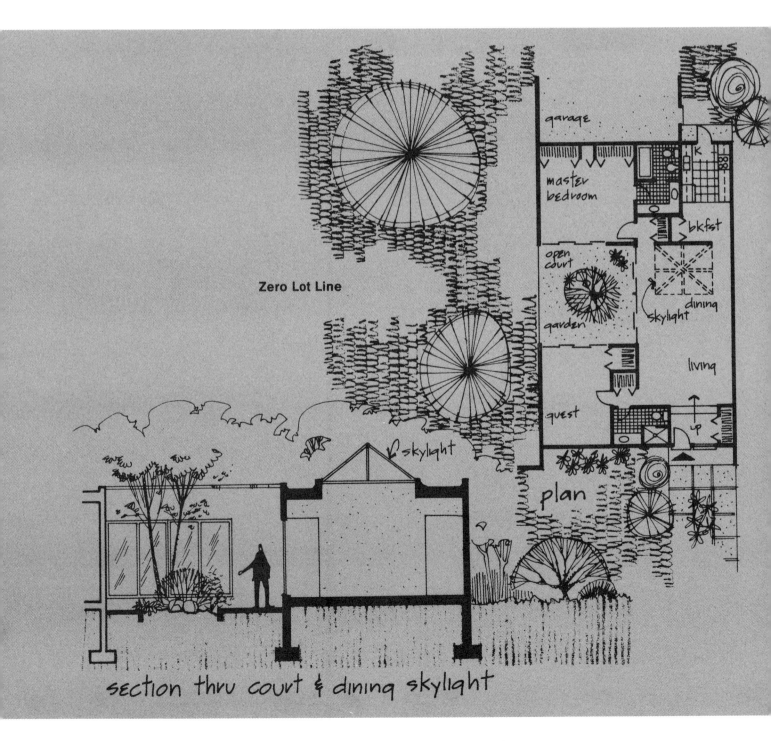

Zero Lot Line

garage

master
bedroom

open
court

garden

guest

k

bkfst

skylight

dining

living

up

plan

section thru court & dining skylight

Zero-lot-line and condominium plans can take on a special kind of livability excitement when three-dimensional space planning is used. In the floor plan and sketch shown, the enclosed courtyard is open to the sky. It gives the feeling of a great volume of space with its unlimited ceiling. The courtyard surface, where paved, should have a continuity with interior flooring to maximize its view extension.

Two bedrooms and main living-dining area all open onto the courtyard. The feeling of extended space can be greatly enhanced when sliding glass doors are run tight against the wall, making the wall seem to extend into the court.

Skylights are another way of giving the extra third-dimension feeling to an interior space. In the example illustrated, the large skylight over the dining area gives the room a sense of extra height, even with an otherwise flat ceiling. The skylight is built up into a clerestory to give a sense of dining space within the living room without other view-blocking breaks or walls.

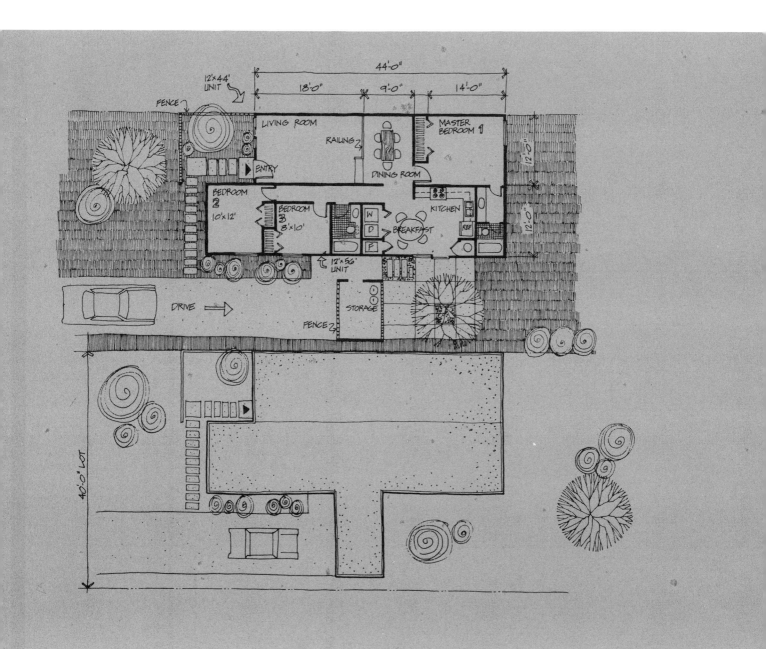

44'-0"

18'-0"   9'-0"   14'-0"

12'x44'
UNIT

FENCE

LIVING ROOM

RAILING

MASTER
BEDROOM 1

DINING ROOM

12'-0"

ENTRY

BEDROOM
2
10'x12'

BEDROOM
3
8'x10'

W
D
F

BREAKFAST

KITCHEN

REF

12'-0"

12'x56'
UNIT

DRIVE

STORAGE

FENCE

40'-0' LOT

6
Designing the Manufactured House

The use of factory built modules for single-family housing allows almost as much freedom for creative design as it imposes constraints in the form of size and economic restrictions. In modular planning, work with the goals of the market involved. Then back into the manufactured module's capacity to solve those market goals. This way, there is maximum freedom to establish new ideas and solutions within the budget, siting and planning restrictions.

Here, for example, a plan for a 40' site with zero side yard provides for the typical three bedroom single-family market, with just enough innovation to be appealing. Yet, the planning takes into account modular economies. All wet (plumbing) requirements are in one unit. There is a minimum of site-built improvements. And there is a minimum of openings in center-joined walls to permit easier shipping.

Note the sunken living area divided by railing from the dining gallery, the family kitchen open to patio for outdoor living, the master bedroom and bath with private view, and the covered fenced garbage-storage area. Vaulted ceilings provide an additional feeling of space within the small rooms.

Relieve the Box Look

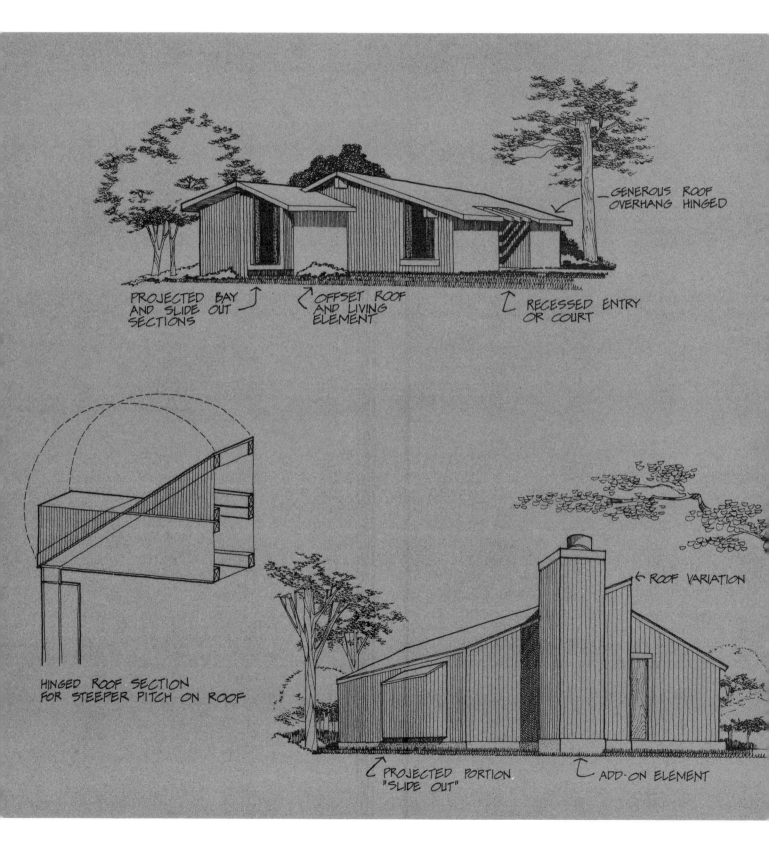

PROJECTED BAY AND SLIDE OUT SECTIONS

OFFSET ROOF AND LIVING ELEMENT

RECESSED ENTRY OR COURT

GENEROUS ROOF OVERHANG HINGED

HINGED ROOF SECTION FOR STEEPER PITCH ON ROOF

ROOF VARIATION

PROJECTED PORTION "SLIDE OUT"

ADD-ON ELEMENT

The sketches of exterior treatments illustrate some of the many ways to achieve relief from the modular box by using factory- and site-applied trimmings.

For steeper roof pitches within the shipping restriction heights, fold the upper roof portion over the lower portion.

For variety on the ends of units, factory-build such elements as projecting privacy blinders, projecting sash units, fireplaces with site-applied chimneys, projecting beam ends.

For long side wall variety, and hinged overhangs, use pre-built boxed bays that can be nailed to interior floors for shipment. Complement the projections with inset areas, such as the recessed entry or courtyard. These could have an open beam roof for additional interest.

The Townhouse Module

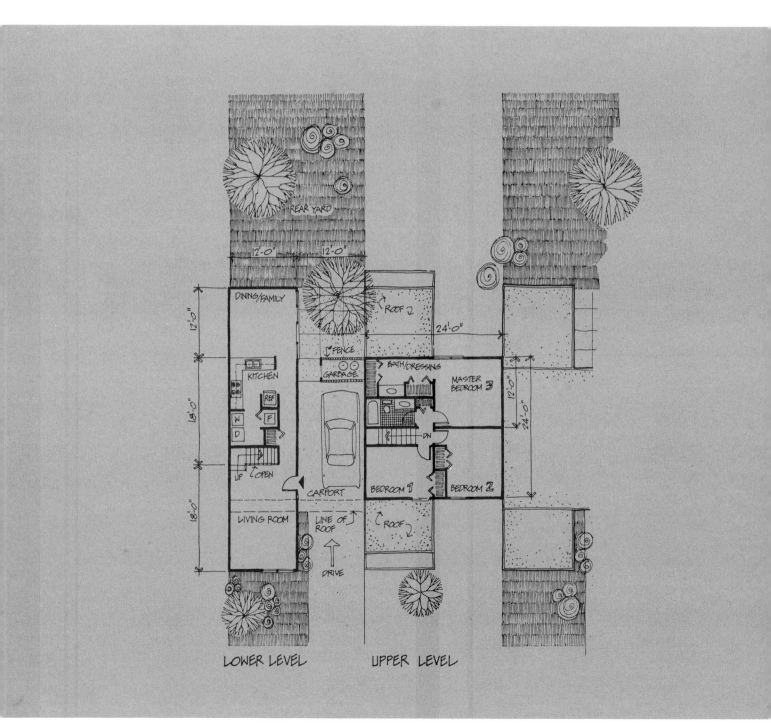

REAR YARD

12'-0" 12'-0"

DINING/FAMILY

ROOF 2

12'-0"

FENCE

24'-0"

BATH/DRESSING

KITCHEN

GARBAGE

MASTER BEDROOM 3

18'-0"

REF

12'-0"

24'-0"

W

F

D

DN

UP OPEN

BEDROOM 1

BEDROOM 2

18'-0"

CARPORT

LIVING ROOM

LINE OF ROOF

ROOF 2

DRIVE

LOWER LEVEL   UPPER LEVEL

Capitalize on freedom to offset modules

One major freedom that modular construction gives to townhouse and garden apartment planning is the economical ability to offset units. Each module is self-structured and supporting. Each unit requires a complete exterior definition. Thus, offsets and projections, cantilevers and grade variations can be added to the design without the usual high cost of conventional construction.

Plan for two-story townhouse (illustrated) uses a lower-level unit 12'x48', and two upper units each 12'x24'. The complete package is a two-trailer load since the upper units can be shipped together on one trailer. Note the interesting living accommodation this configuration gives the individual townhouse unit. At the same time it gives variety of design to the townhouse as a whole.

The lower floor provides covered front entrance, carport and fenced trash area all under the upper-story overhang. Front living room and rear kitchen/family room are well zoned with rear space opening to private outdoor living patio. Upstairs, bath and dressing alcove are in one unit, and three bedrooms need only minimum hall space.

Stacking the Box for Variety

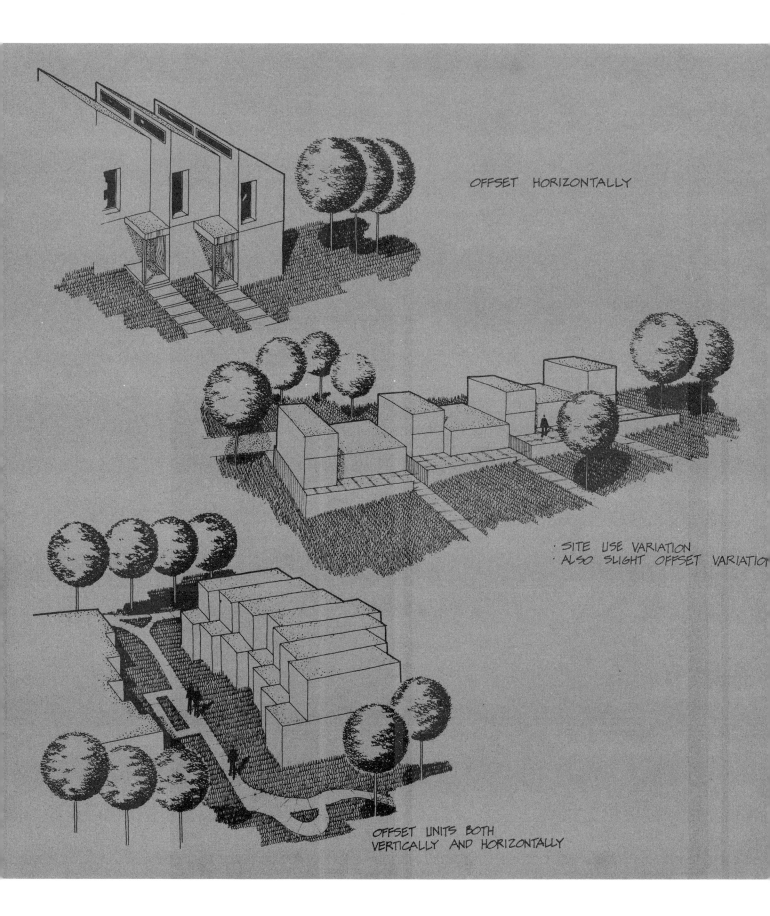

OFFSET HORIZONTALLY

· SITE USE VARIATION
· ALSO SLIGHT OFFSET VARIATION

OFFSET UNITS BOTH
VERTICALLY AND HORIZONTALLY

Break away from rectangular massing

The exterior massing sketches suggest ways to incorporate design variety into inexpensive units. Horizontal offsets retain the intimate residential scale missing in an 8- or 12-unit long single massing. Vertical offsets added to horizontal offset units give additional variation. By using a shorter second-story box for the two-bedroom unit than for the three-bedroom unit, access is provided for the third bedroom's window sash.

Site grade variation is also easily accomplished with boxes since they are basically self-supporting. Combine one- and two-story units and grade variety to make usable those sites which would involve excessive earth moving costs for conventional construction.

Don't think of modular matchboxes all in a row in your planning. Break out of the rectangular massing for more interest, more environmental appeal.

The Luxury Module

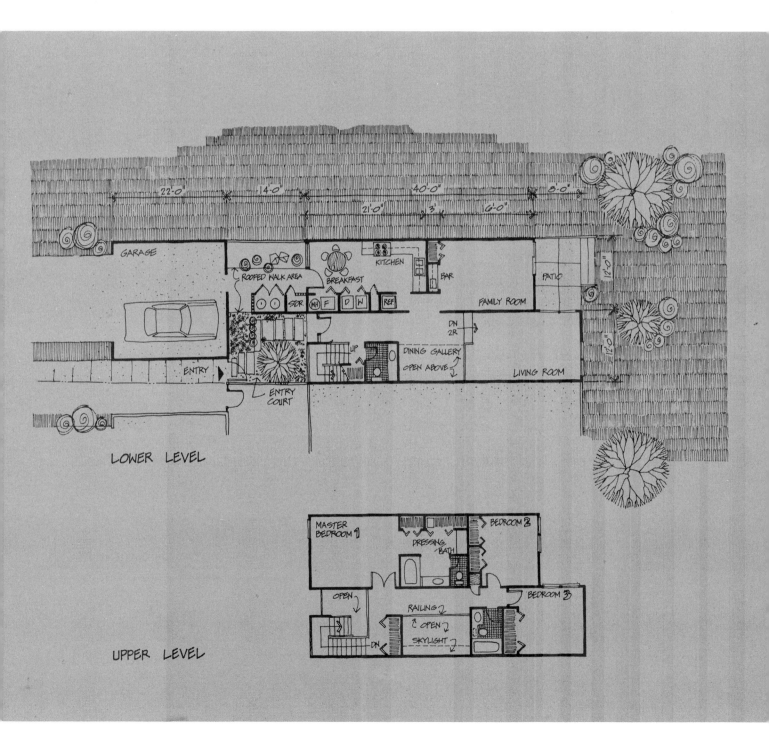

LOWER LEVEL

22'-0"   14'-0"   40'-0"   8'-0"

21'-0"   3'   16'-0"

12'-0"

12'-0"

GARAGE

ROOFED WALK AREA

BREAKFAST

KITCHEN

BAR

PATIO

SDR   WH   F   D   W   REF

FAMILY ROOM

ENTRY

UP

DN 2R

DINING GALLERY

OPEN ABOVE

LIVING ROOM

ENTRY COURT

UPPER LEVEL

MASTER BEDROOM 1

BEDROOM 2

DRESSING BATH

OPEN

RAILING

BEDROOM 3

OPEN

DN

SKYLIGHT

Go to vertical space for the luxury look

The anticipated economies of modular construction and the need for low-cost housing have made this system and this market go hand-in-hand. But the economies that make for planned benefit to low-cost housing may also be well utilized in luxury and/or higher-density planning.

The unit that comprises more individual modules can take advantage of the freedom of vertical space to create a luxurious spaciousness within the limitations of the 12' width. And the high-rise grouping of modular units for more dense housing can take advantage of the inherent structural design of modules, in combination with central utility sources and elevators.

This luxury townhouse plan (illustrated) demonstrates the borrowing of horizontal and vertical space that minimizes the 12' cramps. Entrance is dramatically open to the stair bridge above. Dining area is developed as a gallery with skylighted two-story space along the outer wall. Sunken living room gives greater ceiling height. Kitchen and family areas open to both front and rear patios, one for outdoor living, one for service. Stair bridge seems suspended in space, providing dramatic entrance to master suite. Note emphasis on luxury bath, closet space, privacy of family bedroom wing from balcony views.

The Layered Technique

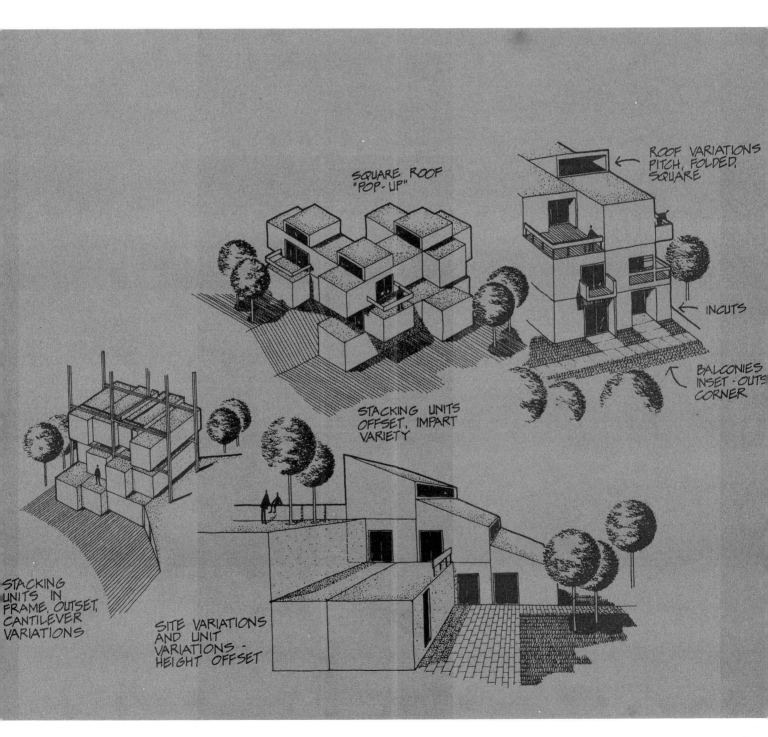

SQUARE ROOF "POP-UP"

ROOF VARIATIONS PITCH, FOLDED, SQUARE

INCUTS

BALCONIES INSET · OUTS CORNER

STACKING UNITS OFFSET, IMPART VARIETY

STACKING UNITS IN FRAME, OUTSET, CANTILEVER VARIATIONS

SITE VARIATIONS AND UNIT VARIATIONS - HEIGHT OFFSET

Use layers of modules for interesting patterns

Where there are several modules per living unit, they can be layered to create interesting patterns (see exterior sketches). If they stack in a structural framework, varying module lengths will give an interesting pattern. If they rest on top of each other, with some units downhill, others uphill, position them in T or L configurations. This will provide private outdoor areas and balconies not only usable as outdoor living areas, but as glamorous views for indoor spaces. Insets and corner breaks will further relieve the visual appearance of cheap "shoeboxes" and give a sophisticated, practical system for building a look of luxury.

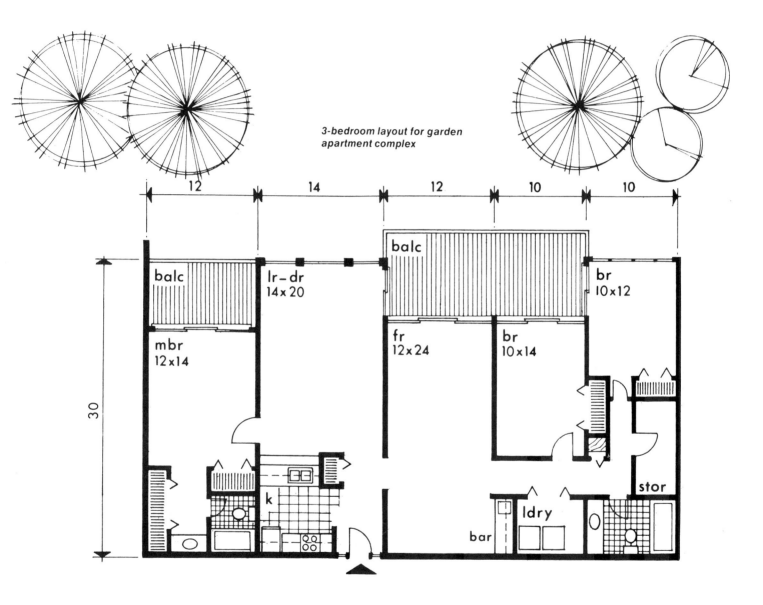

3-bedroom layout for garden
apartment complex

balc

balc

br
10×12

balc

lr-dr
14×20

mbr
12×14

fr
12×24

br
10×14

30

12   14   12   10   10

k

ldry

bar

stor

7
Apartment Planning

**How to eliminate waste, maximize space and dramatize
multi-family living**

Apartments for families with children need the same planning and
zoning appeals as single-family housing today. Informal spaces,
formal rooms, private areas for parents — these replace the tired
living, dining, kitchen threesome.

Here, this typical space for a three-bedroom corridor apartment
tier is well used for contemporary family living. The family room is
grouped with the children's bedrooms for daytime play, evening
family enjoyment. The more formal living room fits adult needs for
a separate living area. The master bedroom is actually an "adult
suite" with a separate dressing room and a private balcony. Even
with these extra amenities, the plan can be adapted to most
multi-family buildings without structural exterior changes.

Go Vertical for Tight Site Space

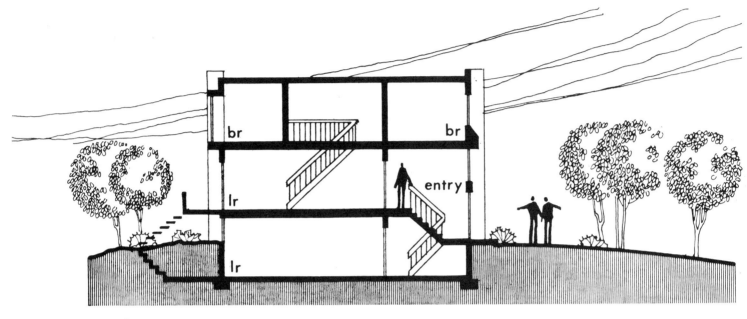

section

Vertical space planning for tight sites

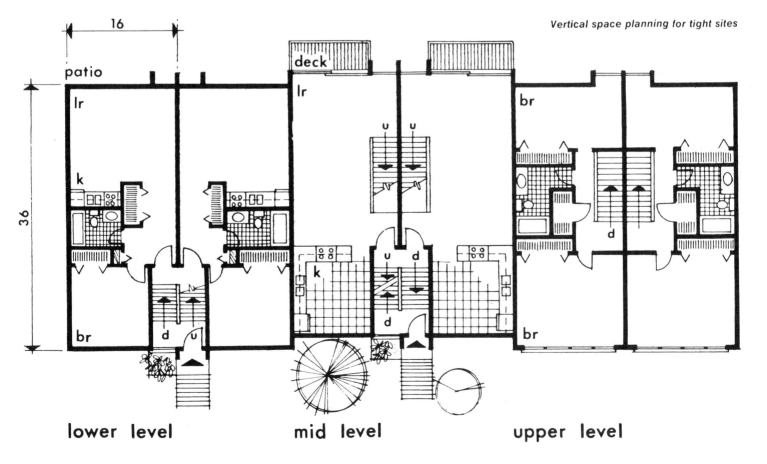

lower level   **mid level**   **upper level**

Vertical space planning for tight sites

The typical 2½-story garden apartment building can have variety and market appeal if space is planned in the vertical as well as horizontal plane. Here the lower level can be either a single three-bedroom apartment or two one-bedroom apartments. Above are two two-bedroom units that live like a townhouse but cost like an apartment.

The upper two-story units are one-half level above the grade entrance. The interior stair in each apartment allows the top level to use the floor space over the entrance. Note the variety of market appeal and unit flexibility this vertical division of space provides, and how it breaks up the typical layered design effect inside and out.

Vertical planning is becoming more important — and imperative — as land prices force the builder to higher densities. But proper utilization of space can take the "multi" out of multi-family even on narrow sites.

Control Vistas and Promote Pleasure

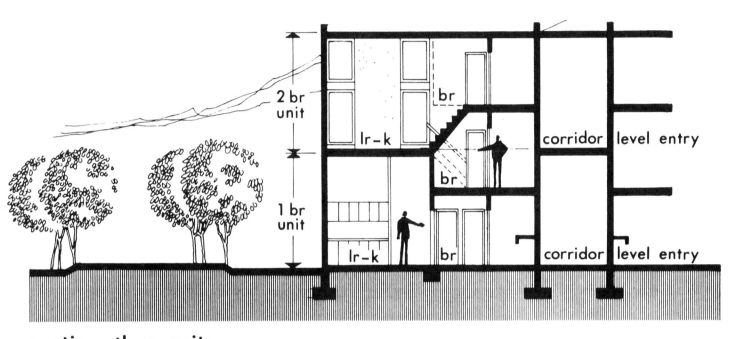

2 br unit

1 br unit

br

lr–k

corridor level entry

br

br

lr–k

br

corridor level entry

section thru units

Two-story rooms have excitement

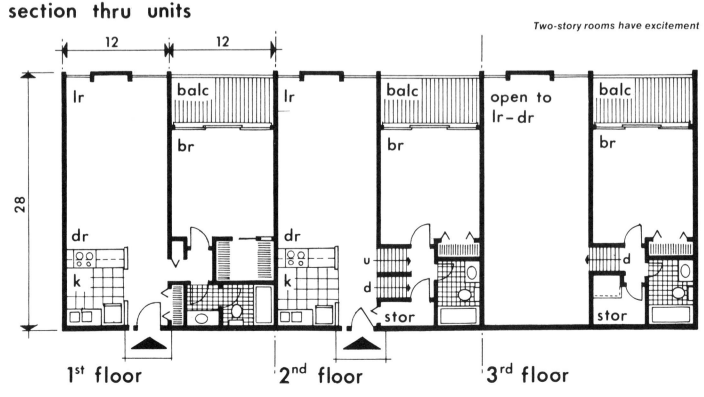

12 12

28

lr balc lr balc open to lr–dr balc

br br br

dr dr u d

k k d

stor stor

1st floor **2nd floor** **3rd floor**

Two-story rooms have excitement

Incorporate the excitement of tall spaces in your apartments. This creates a contemporary sophisticated design which appeals to young marrieds or — with more square footage — to the affluent urban resident who can pay a premium rental.

Here, the living rooms are built as two-story units, each one and one-half stories high. The lower apartment uses a standard height bedroom bay for its one-bedroom plan. The upper apartment uses the double height remaining to create a split-level double-bedroom and bath plan, so ideal for roommates and young families. Note the retention of the mid-level corridor one and one-half flights above exterior grade.

Space Refinements for Townhouses

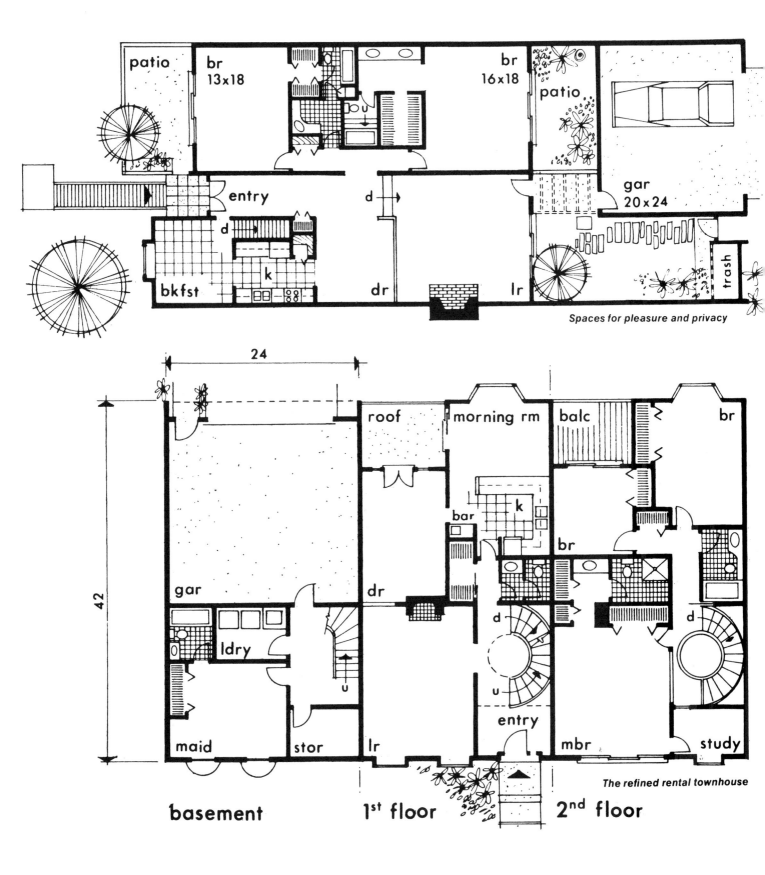

patio

br
13x18

entry

br
16x18

patio

gar
20x24

d

trash

d

bkfst

k

dr

lr

Spaces for pleasure and privacy

24

42

roof

morning rm

balc

br

gar

k

bar

br

dr

d

d

ldry

d

maid

stor

lr

entry

mbr

study

u

u

basement

1ˢᵗ floor

2ⁿᵈ floor

The refined rental townhouse

Spaces for pleasure and privacy

Luxury units need to control as much of their visual environment as possible to create a totally luxurious effect. That means rooms or areas which will give the most personal pleasure and grandeur to the units should be incorporated.

Here is a one-floor 36-ft. wide apartment with rear garage. Note the lavish space devoted to master dressing and walk-in clothing storage room. A completely private master patio and garden allows sunning in seclusion.

Closets and bath should also be somewhat unique in arrangement and treatment to create an impression of the owner's luxurious quarters. Note the large entrance hall with a through vista to the rear wall, the private yard, with covered access to garage, neat-appearing trash area.

Kitchen can be somewhat small, but pantry needs to be large. Breakfast areas should be planned for living for two: desk, comfortable chair, breakfast table.

The refined rental townhouse

The townhouse resident wants his unit to appear as impressive from the outside as the price should indicate. This means keeping automobile circulation away from the front setting which, instead, would appear as a garden walkway. Inside spaces should be scaled for the more formal life that empty-nesters have time and dollars to enjoy.

Here is a two-story-plus-basement townhouse with lower rear garage. The living areas are typical of those found in the more costly houses of the '30s and '40s, the area where much of the rental townhouse market will be moving from.

A stair hall is a unique focal point obviously denoting luxury and the formality of living room's balanced sash, fireplace, adds graciousness and good taste. The rear morning room, with access to the small balcony, gives the family a daily place to live in less formal surroundings.

Townhouse units should do more than just provide additional spaces. The spaces themselves should be refined, the architectural elements uniquely costly in nature, the finishes suggestive of refinement and careful selection.

Turn Space and Site Limitations
to Your Advantage

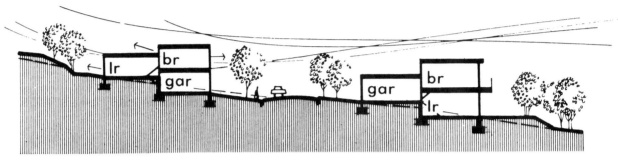

section

Planning the sloping site

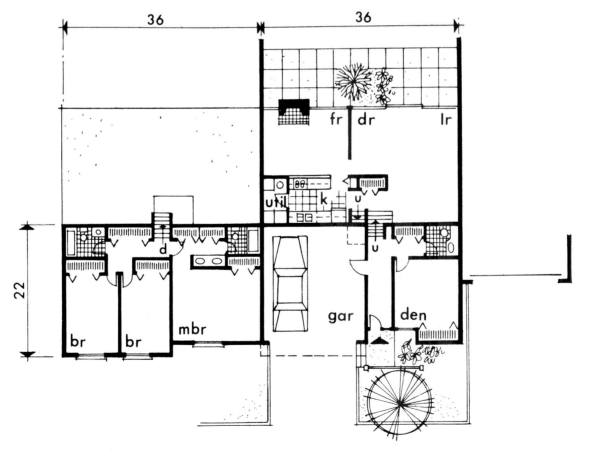

uphill plan

Planning the sloping site

Major space requirements can be applied to sloping land to give maximum benefits with minimum costs. In this example of uphill and downhill houses, the three major planning elements (living areas, bedroom areas, garages) are stacked to lessen grading and excavation costs. This plan also gives easy access and provides outdoor living at grade level.

Note that both houses have garage and entrance level at natural grade. The uphill house steps up one-half flight from entrance to living areas, one-half flight more to bedrooms above garage. The downhill house steps down one-half level from entrance to living areas, one-half level up to bedrooms above living. A den-hobby space and entry garden are interchangeable with either plan.

This change in massing of living areas also adds variety to the streetscape as land slopes change direction.

Plan for a View

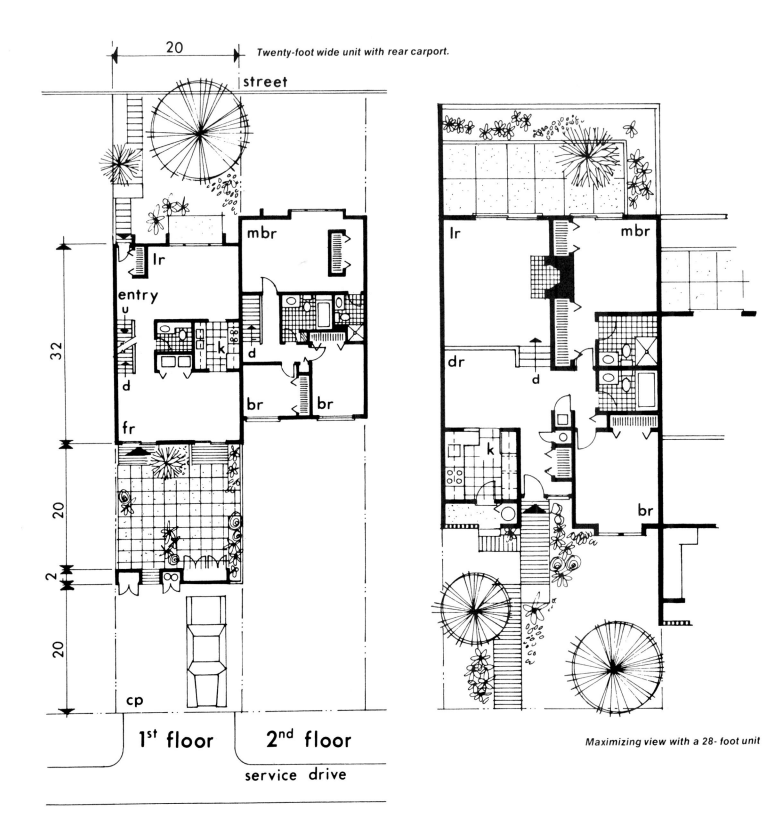

Twenty-foot wide unit with rear carport.

20

street

mbr

lr

entry

u

d

k

d

32

br   br

fr

20

2

20

cp

1ˢᵗ floor   **2ⁿᵈ floor**

service drive

lr   mbr

dr

d

k

br

Maximizing view with a 28-foot unit

Twenty-foot wide unit with rear carport

The old living room-dining room-kitchen syndrome of planning is as outdated for the family townhouse market as it is for single-family houses. Here, more flexible, contemporary living patterns control the plan with formal living to the front street. Informal living to the rear patio.

Note how well this zoning for living can maximize the usefulness of the spaces provided, plus minimize wasted space of non-essential plan elements. A central plumbing core and simplicity of interior plan partitions allow more money for attractive exterior treatment. This also gives variation in setbacks and roof heights, which help give interesting architectural appearance in high-density situations. The plan, in addition, easily incorporates rear outdoor "living courts," carports with storage and trash bin wall.

Maximizing view with a 28-foot unit

Rows of narrow apartment units give a shoebox-like feeling inside if the spaces are not developed to avoid the tunnel effect. Here, for example, in these 28-foot wide one-story units for empty-nesters, rooms are kept as open as possible, yet divided with visual effects to vary interior spaces.

The sunken living room gives a different and more important scale to this space, breaks up the continuous side wall effect without blocking view. A dining balcony has an overlook to maximize the outdoor view. Front kitchen is somewhat separated but not completely closed.

Note the small fence-screened service court with trash bin, the L extension of one side living room wall to give a sense of privacy while retaining view of green space and/or amenities beyond.

sand

bench

patio

wading pool

play deck

tan bark

Playroom

8
Outdoor Living

The ever increasing demand for outdoor living space should be obvious to everyone in the housing industry. But, in spite of this demand, too many of today's homes offer little more than a 4' x 8' slab or deck off the family room.

This tokenism, however, is rapidly disappearing in competitive areas as more builders realize the merchandising power of truly well-planned outdoor living space. Another advantage: "rooms" outside the house are significantly cheaper to provide than they are on the inside.

As the price of land goes up and homes tend to get smaller, it is more important than ever before to squeeze every bit of living space from a lot: to make every room seem larger by extending it outdoors. Some of the ideas that follow should be used in the model as options (to excite buyers about the ultimate possibilities of the home they are about to buy). But most of these techniques are so simple they should be standard.

The important thing is to remember that outdoor living areas must be planned with the same attention and care as the interior; must be thought of as extensions of living functions provided for in the floor plan. In other words, think of outdoor living areas as roofless "rooms" in the true sense of the word, for maximum sales effect.

Playroom. Since most families are motivated to buy their home because of the children, this can be a prime attraction. A portion of the lot (away from the house for noise control, yet in plain view for supervisory reasons) can easily be made into a playground. It can be as simple or elaborate as your market warrants, ranging from a built-in sandbox to a fully equipped play set complete with jungle-jim.

Important considerations are: clear demarcations achieved with plantings, slight changes in level or ground covers. Low maintenance ground covers such as tanbark (indestructible yet non-abrasive) are best. Border ground covers for accent could be ground ivy or myrtle. If decks are used, make certain they are ground level or ramped and guarded. A built-in sand box, recessed in decking, and some simple outdoor storage for toys and tricycles are essential to a functional, outdoor playroom that virtually no buyer has seen.

Outdoor Enticements for Dining

Dining deck

Dining patio

Dining Room. Outdoor dining is probably the most popular use of a deck or patio. To make a deck off the family room seem more important, plan a real dining area. A hole in the deck with a simple pedestal table planted in the middle of it and some cushions on the perimeter, is an easy way to provide permanent outdoor dining space. (No chairs and table to store in winter is a good merchandising point to make.) Built-in cabinets adjacent to the cooking unit not only provide needed storage space for items such as charcoal and cooking utensils, but also furnish some additional counter space for food preparation or serving.

Low voltage and spot lighting are essential since this area is used more often at night than in the day. As with all the outdoor "rooms," the dining area should be defined — made an area separate from the rest of the deck or adjoining patios. One good way to achieve this is with overhead eyelash beams; another, with a simple screen.

Added Function Beyond the Walls

Master Suite

Master Suite. Builders from coast to coast are featuring master suites, and with great success. They usually offer a sitting area as well as dressing room and private bath.

But when there isn't enough space, the bedroom can be extended outdoors. Although complete privacy isn't as necessary as with the sunning spa, it is desirable. A complete enclosure is good, but with a simple partition on one end, shielding it from other outdoor activities will do in many cases. Furnish it for two with an informal seating arrangement. Here again, a telephone and electrical outlet and some accent lighting on plants complete it. To make the bedroom seem larger use more glass (a fixed panel and sliding glass door), and help unify both outdoor and indoor areas with the same outdoor/indoor carpeting. If bedroom is in corner of floor plan, extend the side wall for added visual continuity. This treatment makes it even more difficult to tell where the room ends and outdoors begin.

Space for Relaxing in Sun

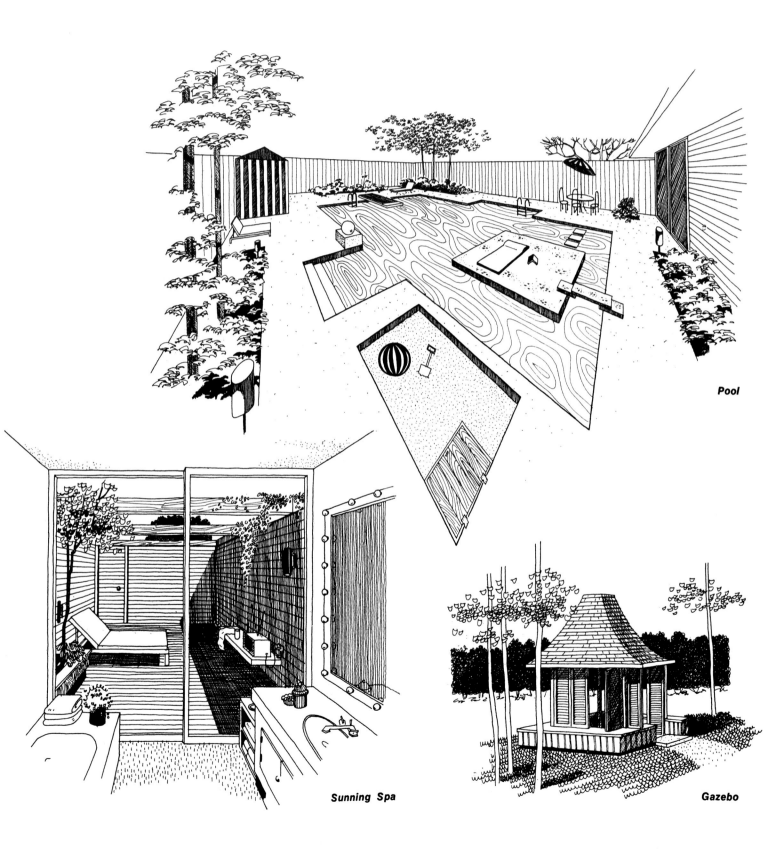

Pool

Sunning Spa

Gazebo

Pool. The ultimate in outdoor living and the last word in status symbols, the swimming pool has taken a few turns for the better. No longer limited to the rectangle, oval or kidney shape, it is now much more than a hole filled with water, a void in the middle of the backyard. New design ideas work it around outdoor living areas, in fact the new irregular shapes create spaces for specific purposes.

Sunning pads which seem to float in the water, small bridges and "entry stairs" transform the pool into an outdoor floor plan, a sparkling watery family room flanked with dining decks, play areas, etc. Not only are the new designs more functional, they are also much more attractive. In the luxury market the additional cost is more than justified.

Sunning Spa. One of the simplest outdoor rooms to create, this requires very little space and adds considerable dimension and excitement to the most ordinary bath. The primary consideration is privacy. A basketweave or louvered fence 8 ft. high surrounding the deck or concrete slab provides complete privacy, yet allows air currents to flow through — an important consideration in small, enclosed spaces.

In warm climates, a partial overhead trellis is a good idea. It provides some shade for reading or plain after-the-shower relaxing.

To complete the "room" approach, install at least one electric outlet for hairdryers, television sets, etc., and a telephone outlet (housed in waterproof box). Low voltage lighting to accent pots of plants or ivy guarantees the patio's dramatic and spatial effect will not be lost at night.

Small bathrooms benefit most from this treatment since any cramped or claustrophobic effect is eliminated. Single or double sliding glass doors may be used, but double, running from wall to wall, add greatest impact. A large mirror on the opposite wall to reflect the patio would make even a 6' x 7' bathroom seem palatial.

Gazebo. Harking back to a 19th Century tradition, the gazebo is a perfect way to create a sense of romance, affluence, and charm. Although more appropriate for larger homes on big lots, simpler, scaled-down versions have begun to crop up for medium priced homes. Its main characteristic: isolation — it's a get-away-from-it-all, free-standing structure. It may or may not be screened and could be shuttered so that in the winter it can be closed, creating storage space for its own outdoor furniture.

Stretch the Floor Plan with Topless Rooms

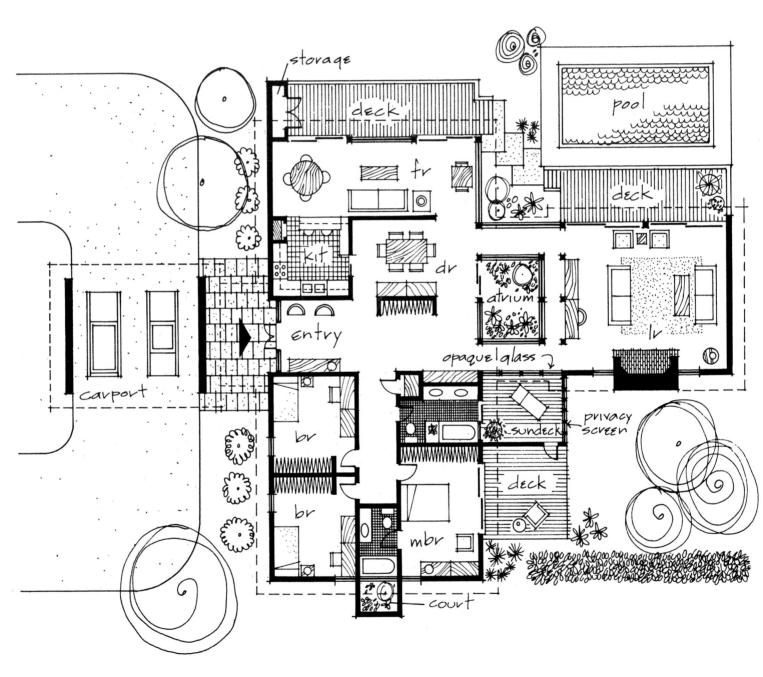

storage

deck

pool

fr

deck

kit

dr

atrium

lv

entry

opaque glass

carport

br

br

sundeck

privacy screen

deck

mbr

court

Total lot living. The floor plan illustrates how good planning relates all active rooms, as well as the master suite, to the outdoors. Considerable square footage of living space is added to this floor plan with three deck "floor extenders." An atrium (either opened or skylighted in colder climates) lifts a chunk of the outdoors and brings it right into the core of the home. No matter where you look in this home, there is a vista, a view of some portion of the lot or atrium. By borrowing space beyond the walls of the home, the floor plan seems vastly extended. Notice also how well all outdoor living areas relate to the rooms within. Proper lighting of all outdoor areas carries space-making benefits into evening hours.

9
Exterior Handling of Doors and Windows

Easy road to variety and style

Doors and windows can make or break your house. With proper planning, they can give your elevation style, character and interest. But lack of planning can reduce an exterior to a dull hodgepodge. What are the rules? This chapter shows how to select, scale and place doors and windows so that the style you want "comes off." Also, it shows how to make several new and interesting elevations from the same basic house plan.

Achieve a traditional design with the same basic house through formal placement of double hung windows, all equally spaced and shuttered. (This example takes some license with the strictly traditional.) Center and flank the double door with sidelights. Two important rules here: never combine two or more double hung windows, and never use a door with a window and sidelights. Either sidelights and solid doors, or a window-door and no sidelights.

Get an informal, rustic treatment with casements, working in harmony with rough-hewn, bolted plank doors. The windows may or may not be leaded, but should be given unity with, for example, a horizontal planter. Here windows are not an intrusion in the brick wall. Planter relates them to the ground. To make window and door style compatible with exterior materials, rough-sawn plywood siding is used for eaves, entry and garage door.

The Contemporary Look and Privacy

Make a contemporary out of the same house with a generous use of glass. A combination of fixed and hopper windows combine to create a glass wall with dramatic vertical thrust. The door treatment is consistent with good contemporary design: it is placed off-center and given importance with two panes of fixed glass to the right. Note how all three elements are tightly organized into one design.

For privacy on a small lot in a high density area, this style answers potential complaints. There's privacy since only a slit window faces the street. Clerestories permit light to flood the living area, and the entry (a flush door with two floor-to-ceiling sidelights) looks out to a private entry court. A privacy screen masks the court from the street. Structurally, the only change you have to make is in the truss system: one side of the roof must be extended to accommodate the clerestories.

Make a Small House Seem Larger

Structural fenestration (A) is one of the most satisfying ways to keep windows from looking like holes poked in the wall. Useful only in contemporary design, windows almost become the total design of the exterior since they are made to follow the structural lines of the house. Spaces are filled with combinations of fixed and movable windows. The danger here is in applying this dramatic treatment to inappropriate sites. Obviously, the view must be meaningful.

The interior layout (B) sometimes demands an awkward combination of windows and doors. For example, a master bedroom with a balcony may be next to another room with a different kind of fenestration. On the exterior, these different elements can be combined with a strong structural treatment. Here the roof overhangs the entire cluster, enveloping windows and doors in a single unit. Horizontal balcony railing slats complete the job of unifying.

A small house (C) can present the problem of too many "breaks." In other words, too many small windows chop up the elevation, making the house appear even smaller than it is. Solution: move these windows closer together when possible and then tie them together with bold framing so that they take on the appearance of a single design unit. Try to repeat the framing motif at the entry or garage.

Windows with Dimension and Character

The trend to outdoor living (D) has done more to eliminate the barriers between "in and out" than anything since the invention of glass. Most of the efforts are directed toward opening the indoors to gardens or vistas. Here's an example of dramatically bringing the outdoors in. Recessed floor to ceiling sliding glass doors eliminate walls altogether. Therefore two patios, or "porches" are totally integrated with the interior.

Ordinary windows (E) may be given dimension and character by projecting the structure around them. A shadow box effect is easily created by bringing the roof line slightly over the whole unit together with side frames and window boxes. Do this only when other design elements in the elevation echo the same modular feeling.

Add character (F) to small windows by surrounding them (in a traditional home) with interesting framing. Here, French windows break the roof line and add dimension to an otherwise flush elevation. The result is formal, yet warm. This is also an excellent solution for townhouses where large expanses of unbroken brick can spell monotony.

Select the First Key to Authentic Design

When your buyers step up to your house, the entry door immediately sets the tone of everything else you offer. Doors should be given the most careful consideration to blend with the total style of the house, and serve as a focal point. Whether they are rustic, provincial, georgian, or contemporary, every detail must be integrated and work toward a total idea.

If there are massive solid doors (upper left), relieve them with sidelights, and frame them with equally massive structural members. If the door is provincial (above) keep everything else balanced and formal. Contemporary homes (below) are usually asymmetrical, but must be tied together to create a single design element.

10
Interior Handling of Doors and Windows

Add character to large and small rooms
The preceding chapter explored various exterior effects that can be created with the proper handling of doors and windows. This chapter focuses on interior effects: how windows can emphasize and compliment architectural features, how doors can help solve difficult design problems, and how both can be used to give your interiors a special touch. This is the finished look that often spells the difference between sale and no sale.

Cathedral ceilings and sunken living rooms are enjoying great popularity all over the country. But they present a challenge. Ordinary window treatments seem out of place, lost in the greater vertical spaces they create.

The cathedral ceiling on the left is accented with two floor-to-ceiling windows flanking the fireplace. Tall, slender proportions of the windows add greatly to the sense of height created by the open cathedral ceiling. And, as a bonus, the two windows create a summer focal point for the furniture grouping facing the fireplace.

Blending Indoors and Outdoors

Put merchandising punch into your kitchen by "attaching" a garden. It's really nothing more than an ordinary kitchen with pass-through to the patio. The usual over the sink kitchen window is expanded counter-to-ceiling, wall-to-wall, and a ledge replaces the usual sill. In warm climates the concept can be extended to another wall where 8 ft. sliding glass doors open onto pool or garden.

Bring a small, enclosed and private patio inside the bathroom itself with a garden bath. This is one of the new hot buyer features on the West Coast. Not only does a garden bath reduce the often claustrophobic feeling of many bathrooms, but it also floods it with light, improves ventilation, and adds a dimension of luxury. In this sketch, one wall is replaced with a sliding glass door and one fixed window. In colder climates where this would be impractical, a similar effect is possible with one fixed floor to ceiling window, and a privacy screen around a small patio or pot garden.

Dramatize sunken living rooms with a large clerestory over a wall of sliding glass doors. The result is a very spacious and airy look. Although appropriate in any size home, this treatment is particularly useful when smaller townhouse living rooms face a rear garden. The added height and glass create an illusion of more space.

Smooth Over the Choppy Look
and Build in Drama

Blend indoors and outdoors with entry windows and bright light into a dark foyer as well as the living areas beyond. The clerestories running across the top are carried through into the front hallway leading to the bedrooms. With an open plan such as this one, it is advisable to provide some kind of partitioning between the entry and living room. A change in level (one step down into the living room might do it) or a railing such as the one used here is just enough to define the area. It also "steals" the space and light for the living area.

Door Solutions to Trouble Spots

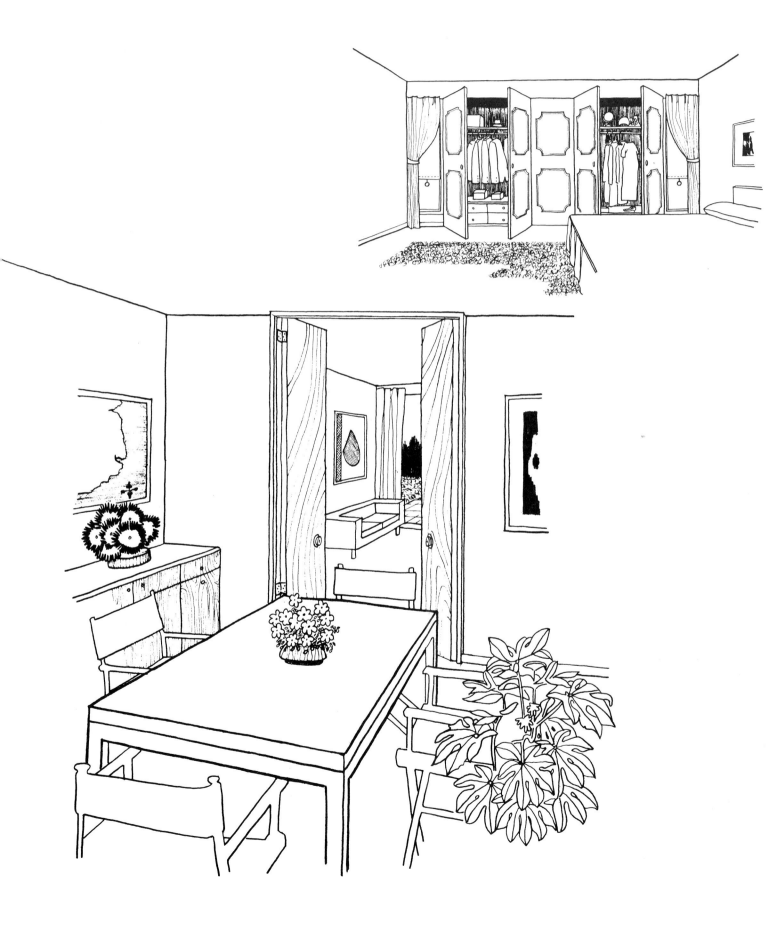

Solve difficult interior design problems with — doors. For example, many master suites look "choppy" because wall is often broken by "his" and "hers" closets and an access door. This choppiness can be camouflaged with fixed matching doors between the breaks.
To reduce costs, it works particularly well with stock paneled doors. When closet doors are shut, a design liability is transformed into a solid, richly paneled feature wall.

Build up drama with tall doors. Standard 8 ft. double doors may be used to gain a sense of formality and elegance. Formal dining rooms, in great demand again, become more important when given this entrance treatment. Trim door at sides and top with 1″ x 1″ square mouldings and make sure that the door is about ¼″ below ceiling, especially if using accoustical spray.

How Interior Effects Can Create That Finishing Touch

Solve the foyer problem. Foyers are often a floor plan nightmare because closet doors, living room access openings, and hallways converge to create a design muddle at that point where clutter is least desirable. An entry is, after all, a first impression of a house. Handsome wallcoverings or decorating tricks often don't work because the area is too broken up. They tend to accent the divisions rather than smooth them over.

Stock doors, if used in combination of fixed and movable arrangements, can neatly cover problem foyers. As seen here, the result is a rich and inviting paneled entry rather than an abrupt clash of materials.

Give an authentic finished look to dining rooms in traditional homes. Mount paneled doors horizontally along the walls, (these are stock Ponderosa Pine doors) and finish off with simple crown chair mouldings. The effect of deep dimensional wainscoting adds considerable architectural interest to what otherwise might be a rather plain room.

Cheerful and Flexible

Cheer up breakfast areas or eating facilities in a family room by creating a bay with stock French doors. In the sketch here, four doors are fixed and the two center doors are hinged and lead out into the patio. The divided light bay creates a warm and informal effect, and certainly provides the room with a memorable focal point. Woodsy tones in paneling and ceiling beams complete the rustic, country look.

Add flexibility to a small house floor plan with louvered doors. These are particularly useful when space has been stolen from the formal living room for the family room. Doors may be used to completely enclose the area, or partially divide and therefore define each room.

If placed on tracks they may be completely opened when entertaining large numbers of people, or closed when various family activities require privacy.

When a family room opens on a patio and, therefore, is an open and airy room, louvered doors provide the touch of texture and enclosure.

KITCHENS

Designs with the market in mind

A Gourmet Center of Action

11
Kitchens

The sketches offer kitchen design suggestions for luxury single-family homes. On the following pages in this chapter some of these same planning principles are applied to less costly kitchens in smaller houses, townhouses and apartments.

A gourmet center of action is provided when the kitchen is designed for casual living and entertaining (left). Here, food delivery from garage is first brought to a litter counter, then to the pantry for bulk storage, and finally to the kitchen for small-item storage.

Inner kitchen, concealed from family room view, is for basic preparation prior to family and guest participation. Open outer area, with bar and cook-top barbecue, is for final flourishes.

Note convenience of both refrigerator and freezer to food storage and use. Trash compactor is at rear entry. At the bar is an ice maker and a second dishwasher for party clean-up. Maple chopping block covers the entire countertop in party kitchen.

Stepsavers and Viewmakers

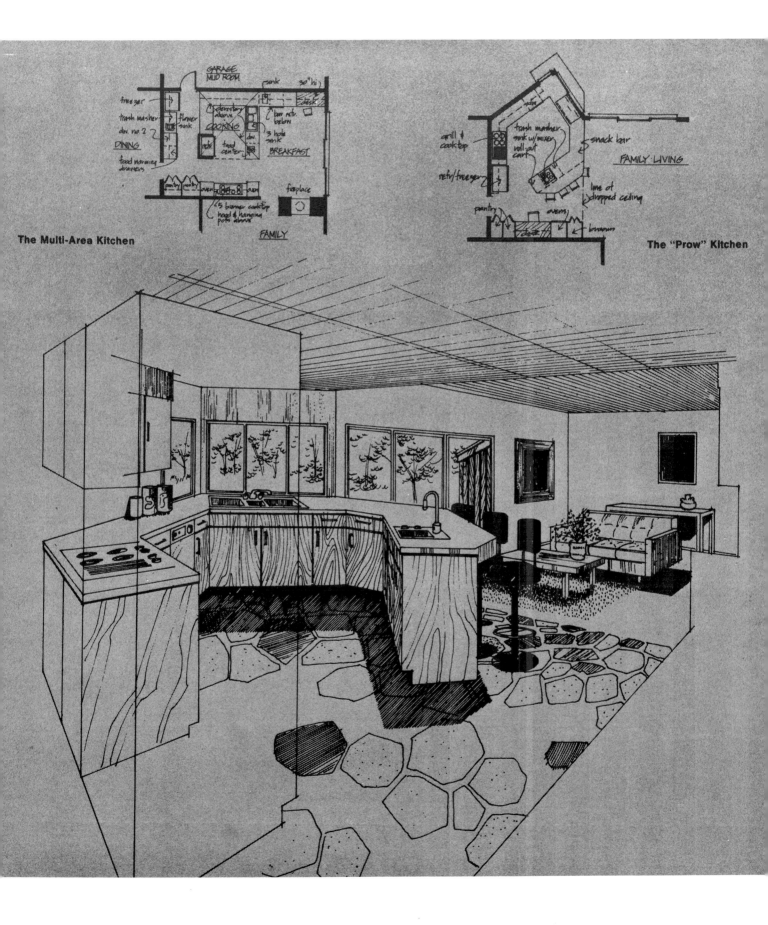

The Multi-Area Kitchen

The "Prow" Kitchen

The multi-area kitchen (far left) is designed to make both everyday family meals and larger entertaining meals convenient. Adequate storage is built into double pantry cabinets adjacent to unloading counter, convenient to both food delivery and usage. Extra sink and second dishwasher let this area double for flower arranging, party serving, etc.

Small basic kitchen area saves steps and time for everyday meals. Note minimum traffic disruption and clerestory lighting. Rear area extends counter for bar and desk use nearer family room. Cabinets are built along perimeter walls only, to give freer, open feeling to room. Breakfast room overlooks garden, shares view and conversation with chef.

A "prow" kitchen, with projection extending beyond the side walls of the house, offers the excitement of indoor-outdoor design. Here, an offset angle brings the sink and counter right out into the garden-patio.

Cabinetry is kept simple so as not to compete with the outdoor scene. Sash is brought right down to counter, and counter is extended outside at same level for exterior eating bar. To give full open feeling, glass is returned at tip of prow at least to depth of counter. Glass area is continued into family room for same reason. Various counter depths, two feet at cabinets, wider at snack bar, also contribute to flowing spatial feeling of room.

Corridor area by kitchen incorporates less frequently used but vital requirements: pantry and broom cabinets, double ovens, desk surface and storage. More frequent meal preparation needs are within traffic-free open "U": refrigerator-freezer, cooktop with built-in barbecue, sink and dishwasher, extra party sink with built-in mixer.

Mid-priced Kitchens with Luxury Ideas

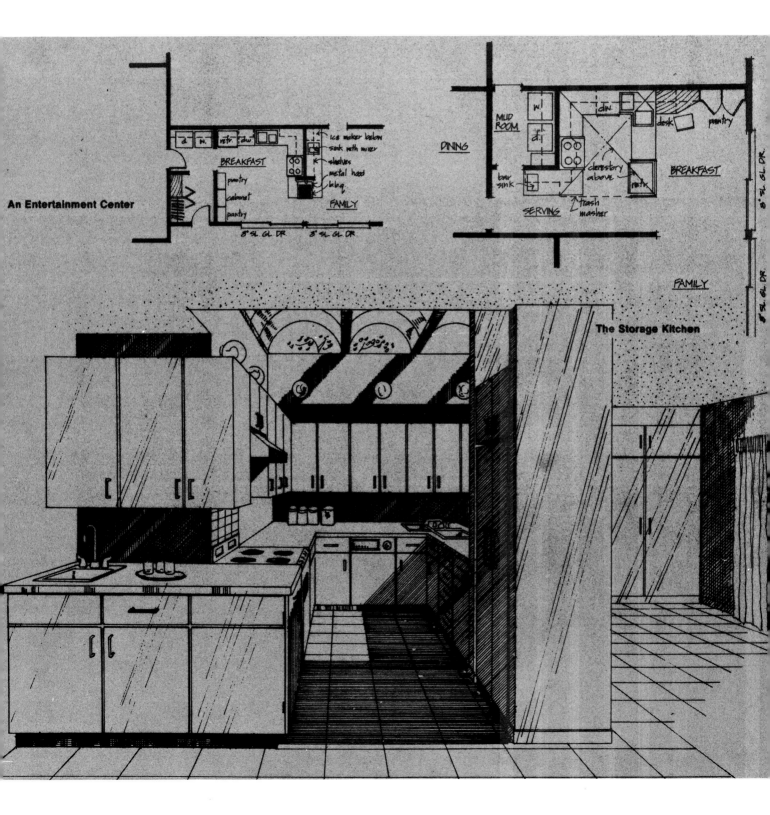

An Entertainment Center

BREAKFAST

FAMILY

pantry
cabinet
pantry

ice maker below
sink with mixer
shelves
metal hood
bbq.

8' SL. GL DR   8' SL. GL. DR

DINING

MUD ROOM

bar sink

SERVING

w

dr

dw

clerestory above

trash masher

desk

pantry

BREAKFAST

refr.

FAMILY

The Storage Kitchen

An entertainment center, including food and drink preparation areas, in a home of usual size is also possible. Plan (top, left) incorporates both coat and pantry closet in mud/laundry room. Inner kitchen/breakfast room is an efficient "L" shape, with bonus 12-in. deep pantry and counter-height cabinets along side wall.

Decorative barbecue is built into end divider wall and vents through same duct as adjacent range. Party and buffet counter continues around to bar area with sink and ice maker.

A storage or multi-area kitchen can incorporate many "big" ideas in limited space. Main cooking "U" at left is convenient and workable, brightly lighted by clerestory or skylight above.

Counter continuation around corner becomes party serving and bar area. Small desk is built into corner continuation next to breakfast room. Pantry cabinets here provide for storage of seldom-used items.

Cabinets, in fact, are used only on perimeter walls. Note the rather minimum use of small wall cabinets and the maximum use of full height units which store more in easy-to-see view. Divider at refrigerator-freezer makes minimum break. Open feel is maximized even though cabinet space is generous.

Corner sink allows view over island and makes use of an otherwise difficult cupboard well.

Glass and Greenery Appetizers

The Greenhouse Kitchen

The greenhouse kitchen (left) incorporates a small plant area right into the projection foundation. Area is designed as a continuation of the counter-high sash, with access from the family room for plant care.

Kitchen has frequent-use appliances in the traffic-free "U" shape for minimum steps and disruption. Snack bar is at counter height for a continuous open feeling. Cabinets, counters and appliances should be selected with blending, rather than contrasting, colors. This will allow the garden to add its decoration without making the room seem "too busy."

Bar, desk area and double oven divider cabinet are built into opposite wall along traffic route.

Mini Kitchens with the Emphasis on Glamour

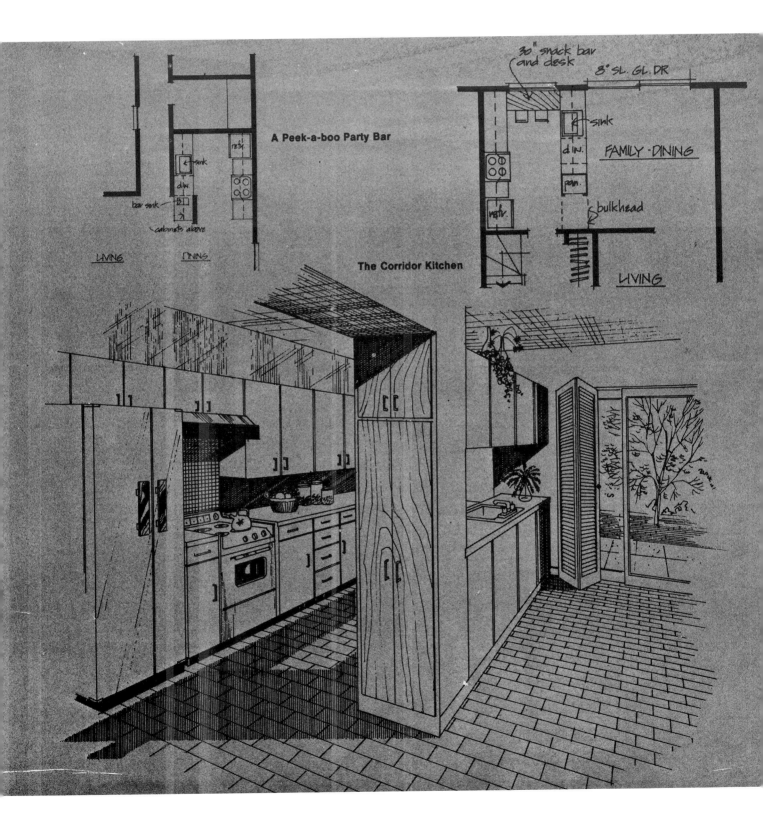

A Peek-a-boo Party Bar

30" snack bar and desk

8' SL. GL. DR

sink

refr.

FAMILY · DINING

sink

d.w.

d.w.

bar sink

pan.

cabinets above

refr.

bulkhead

LIVING

DINING

The Corridor Kitchen

LIVING

A peek-a-boo party bar (plan, far left) is possible even in small apartment and townhouse kitchens, with careful planning. As shown, a party bar sink is incorporated into the sink counter, with divider wall offset in such a way as to block the view of the cooking area while retaining pass-through for convenience. Cabinets above bar sink are of the same design as other kitchen cabinets.

Simple addition of the offset wall and party sink provides whole kitchen area with feeling of better planning and more kitchen enjoyment. Meal preparation and drink preparation can be done simultaneously even in relatively confined space.

A corridor kitchen (left) provides very adequate facilities in a space just eight feet wide. Continuation of the counter across the end of the corridor space, either as a desk or for eating, gives double use to the area. It also visually connects the two sides of the cabinets, for a much larger, more continuous look to the kitchen plan.

With upper cabinets held above eye level, island sink counter opens view to the family room. If there is no possibility of glass in the kitchen, an adjacent family room sliding glass door will provide daytime illumination. Good under-cabinet lighting is a must.

Built-in pantry at the end of the divider wall provides much needed storage space. Unit also serves to divide family and kitchen spaces without cramping or blocking the view.

Small Projection, Big Space

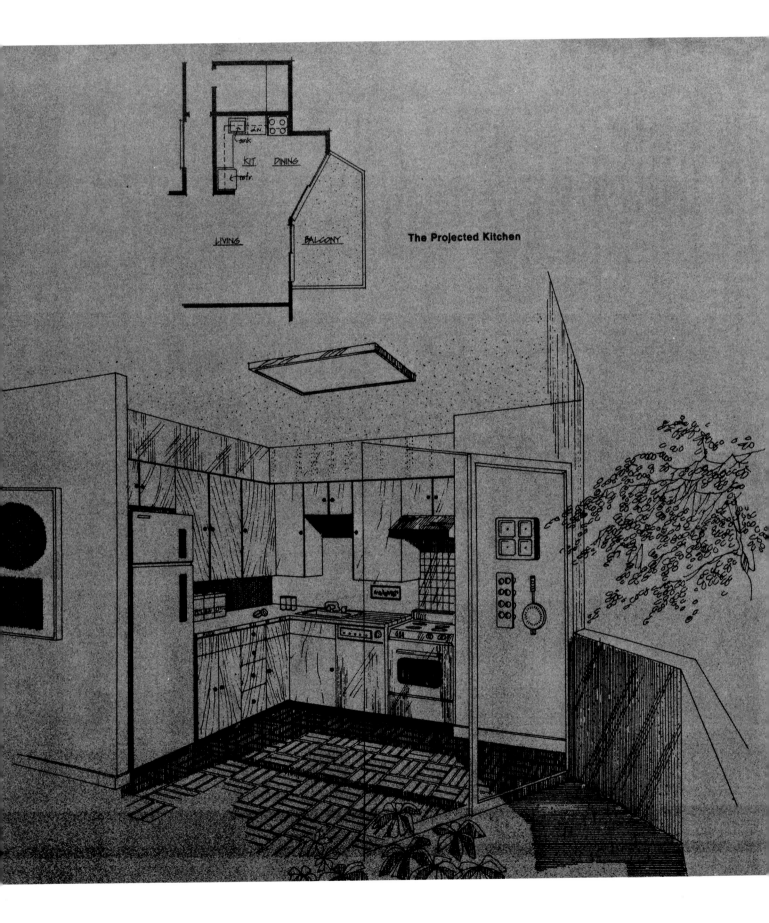

KIT. DINING

sink

refr.

LIVING BALCONY

The Projected Kitchen

The outward projection of this kitchen plan (left) makes way for a breakfast-dining space. Small kitchen "L" is built along the inner wall and a dining area is created within the extension.

Projection creates a private viewing pocket from the inside and extra balcony or patio seclusion from the outside. Continuation of the glass wall into the sliding glass doors of the living room provides spatial expansion, making the balcony or patio act as an extension of the inside rooms.

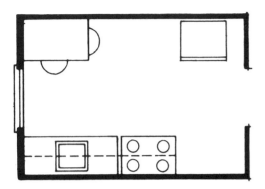

before

after

Small apartment kitchen

12
Kitchen Remodeling

Design recipes to stretch space and storage

Apartment kitchens that are "dead-ended" make perfect U-shaped kitchens because all wall space can be put to use. Even when the room is fairly narrow (here about 8 ft.), the U-shape is possible because one wall can be made up of 11″ overhead cabinets instead of the usual 24″ base cabinets. These cabinets may be wall mounted just like overheads or placed on a frame resting on the floor.

A small eating space is created by turning a portion of the counter perpendicular to this wall.

Widening the doorway relieves spatial tension and appears to widen the whole room. Bifolds or accordian doors may be installed on tracks if living area is immediately adjacent to the kitchen.

Kitchen carpeting, dark stained cabinets, colorful vinyl wallcoverings and suede-finished plastic laminate countertops make it an attractive, "live-in" kitchen.

The Efficiency

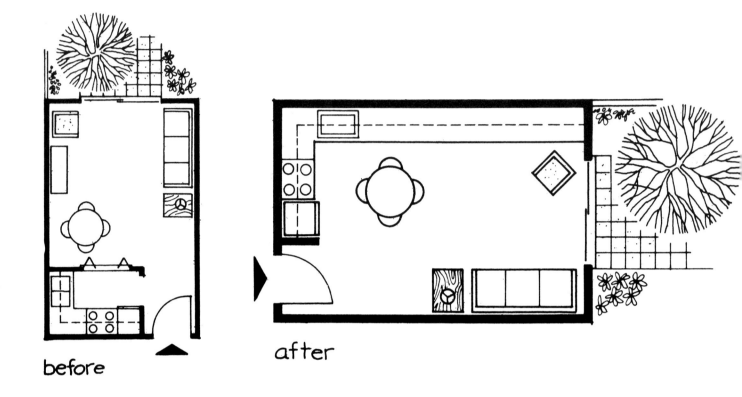

before

after

The efficiency kitchen

An efficiency apartment usually has a small L-shaped kitchen that defies expansion or re-planning. But with the new, non-kitchen products and materials and some subtler lighting, the old kitchen can be brought right into the living area.

Result is that both the cooking and living areas seem larger and less confined in a small apartment. Also, storage is greatly enhanced (a chronic complaint of apartment dwellers), and the apartment is semi-furnished making it much more desirable to the younger tenant who is usually attracted to this kind of unit.

The partition is removed and cabinets are continued along one wall of the living room.

Handsome walnut-finished cabinets combined with coppertone appliances that blend into the cabinetry are best. Plastic laminate countertops in new living-room finishes such as black leather give the entire area a warm, living-room look.

Overhead lighting should be removed and replaced with under-the-cabinet counter light. Kitchen area should be under separate control so it can be de-emphasized when not in use.

Solving Three Problems
by Shifting the Work Triangle

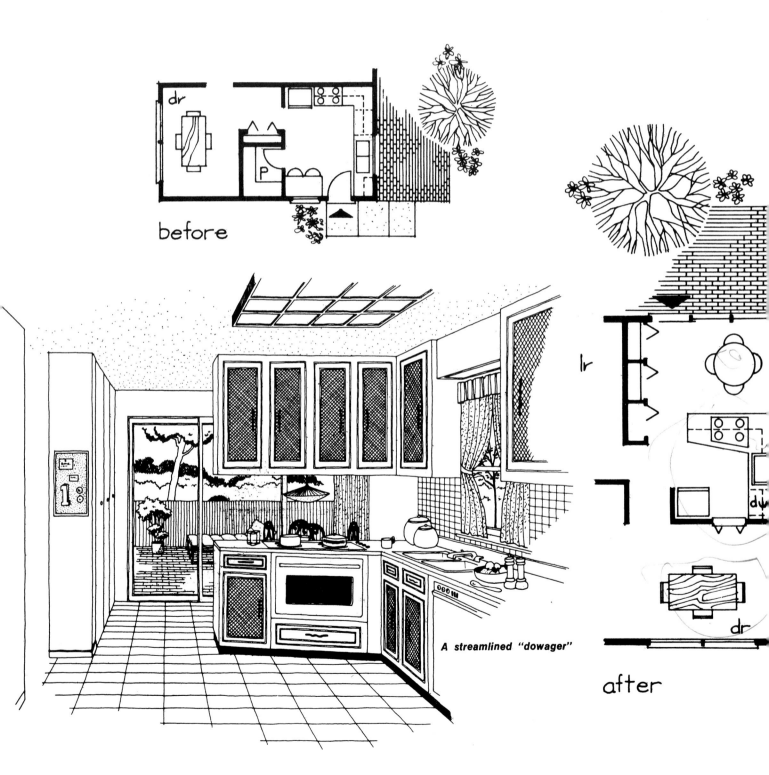

before

A streamlined "dowager"

after

Large, old homes often separate the kitchen area and the dining room with large halls and pantry space. The result is that serving in the dining room is an exhausting experience. These old homes also usually have bad traffic flow, directing family traffic through the work area, and kitchen eating space is badly organized.

All three problems may be solved by moving the work triangle to the middle section where the pantry once was. This frees some really usable space for kitchen dining and places the housewife squarely between the formal and informal dining areas for greater convenience to both. Traffic is also routed around the work area.

A pantry wall stores more than the old, poorly organized pantry, and sliding glass dooors opening on a deck flood the kitchen with light and garden view.

Island Is Problem Solver

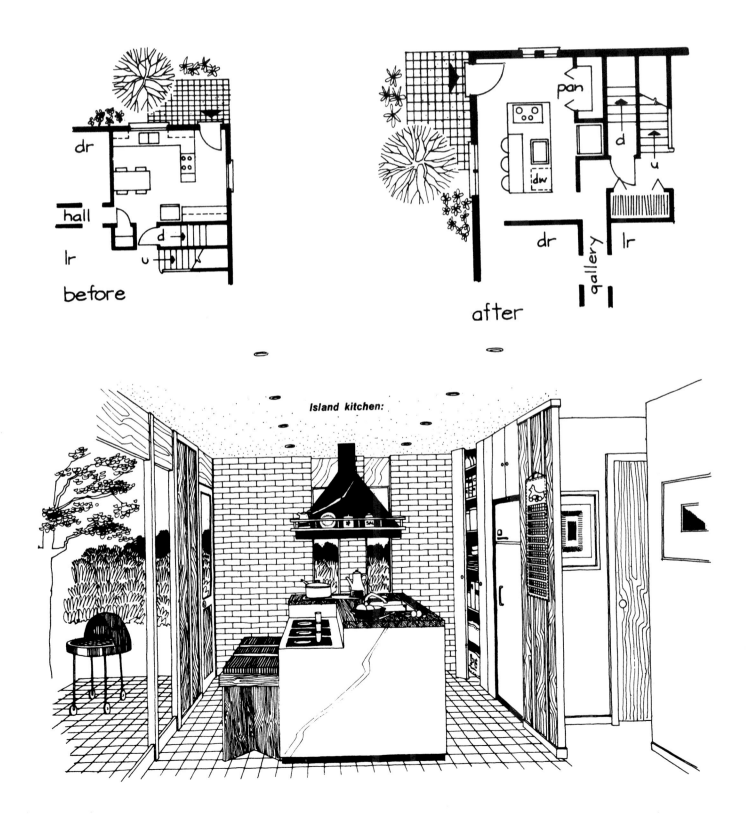

dr

hall

lr

before

pan

dr

gallery

lr

d

u

after

Island kitchen:

Kitchens with too many openings are difficult to plan because of the fragmented wall space. When it is impossible or impractical to remove some of the doors and windows, a good solution is to provide an island kitchen. Surface burners, oven, sink and dishwasher can be housed in a large core that will also offer eating area and food preparation space. Refrigerator is housed on the unbroken wall. Traffic is directed to the opposite side of the island leaving the work triangle unencumbered.

The worktop may be butcher block with a portion of it dropped to dining height. A gourmet kitchen effect can be achieved with overhead hoop for hanging pots and utensils.

Storage Walls and Garden Nooks
from 20-Year-Old Kitchens

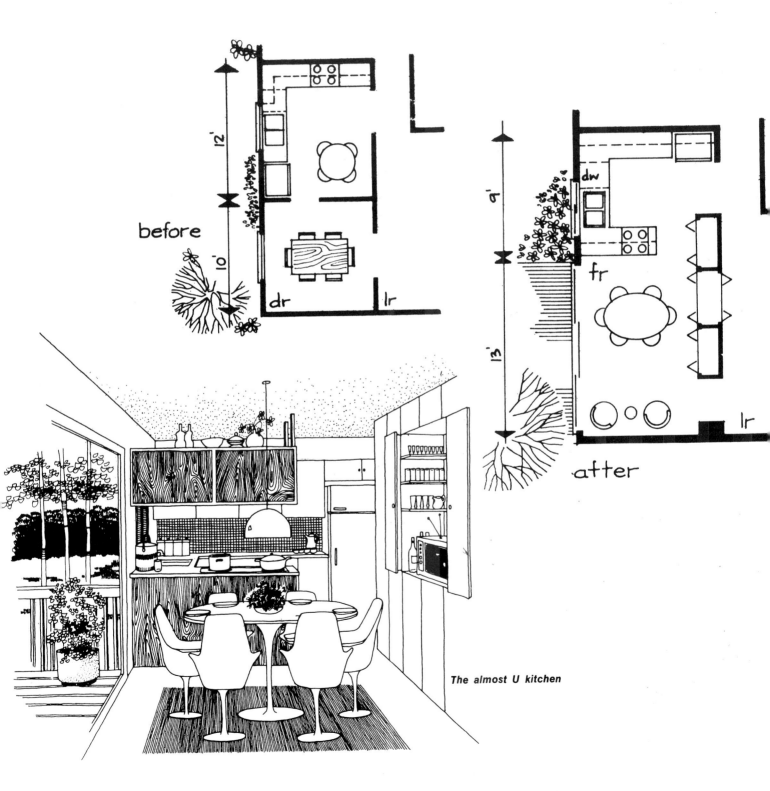

before

12'

10'

dr   lr

9'

dw

fr

13'

lr

after

The almost U kitchen

The typical post-World War II house had a close kitchen/dining room relationship, but both were too small to be truly enjoyable.

By removing the old partition between them and reorganizing the new, larger space, a new informal living area is created. There's more room for family dining. A storage wall with a pass-through separates this informal area from the living room.

The old L-shaped kitchen is closed into a partial U, with overhead cabinets between kitchen and family room. Sliding glass doors replace window, and a deck extends the family room into the garden.

Putting Porch to Work

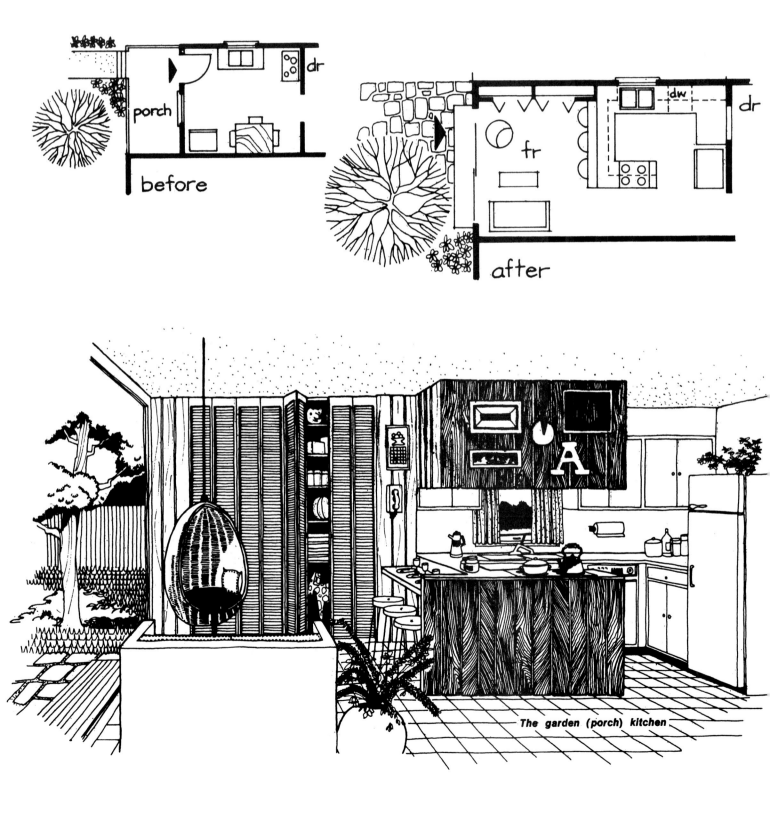

porch

dr

before

dw

fr

dr

after

The garden (porch) kitchen

The old back porch is, more often than not, wasted. Little indoor/outdoor relationship makes it nothing more than a place to pile up bicycles and garden tools.

But it is valuable space which can be turned into useful family sitting space with garden kitchen motiff.

The old traffic pattern dragged through the center of the kitchen to the back door. The new plan routes traffic alongside the work area.

Sliding glass doors glaze in the rear of the old porch, and a storage wall runs in front of the new outside wall. This allows for eating space, sitting space and a garden view.

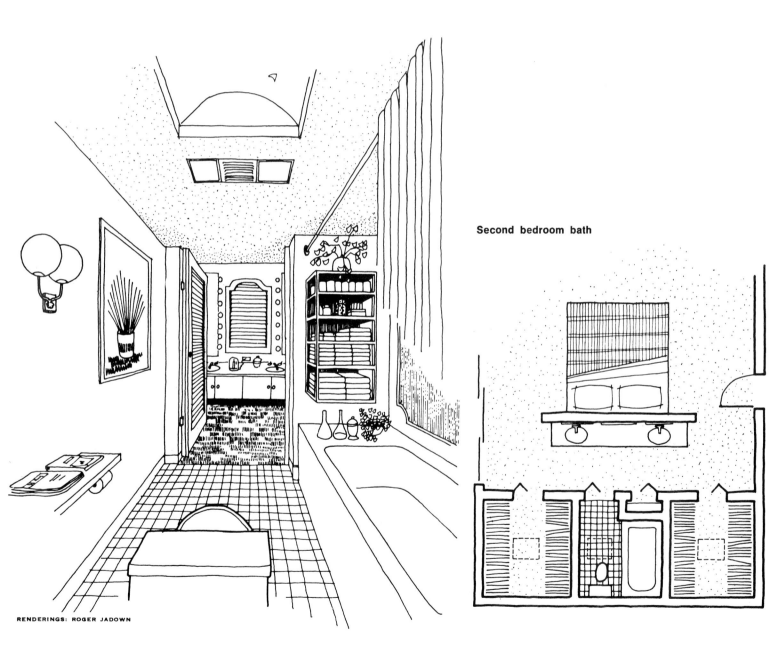

Second bedroom bath

RENDERINGS: ROGER JADOWN

13
Second Bath Need Not Be Second Best

Second and third baths are no longer uncommon in today's homes. The latest available research shows that over 50% of the best selling models have two or more baths.

But too often the first bath gets all of the attention — gold faucets, razzle-dazzle wallcoverings, rich carpeting, mirrors and vanities — while the second bath scrapes by with the bare minimum three fixtures (or just two) crammed into an awkward space.

Following are some ideas to help your second or third bath "work harder."

A second bedroom private bath is always a problem because of lack of space. That's because the lion's share of the bedroom zone is usually turned over to the master suite. Assuming the second bedroom is of average size and not cramped, space can be stolen from the bedroom itself for the vanity or vanities, behind a partition which also serves as a headboard for the bed. By moving the sink into the room, a small closet-like space may be allotted to the second bath for tub or shower and water closet.

However, a few design concepts are necessary to relieve any claustrophobic tensions. First, a skylight. This will open the room and draw the eye to its full height, emphasizing cubic space rather than just square footage. Second, double louvered doors carried up to the ceiling will help bedroom and bath spaces blend more successfully. Third, a light fixture at the end of the room will balance the light and make the room seem wider.

Count on Corners and Double Duty Space

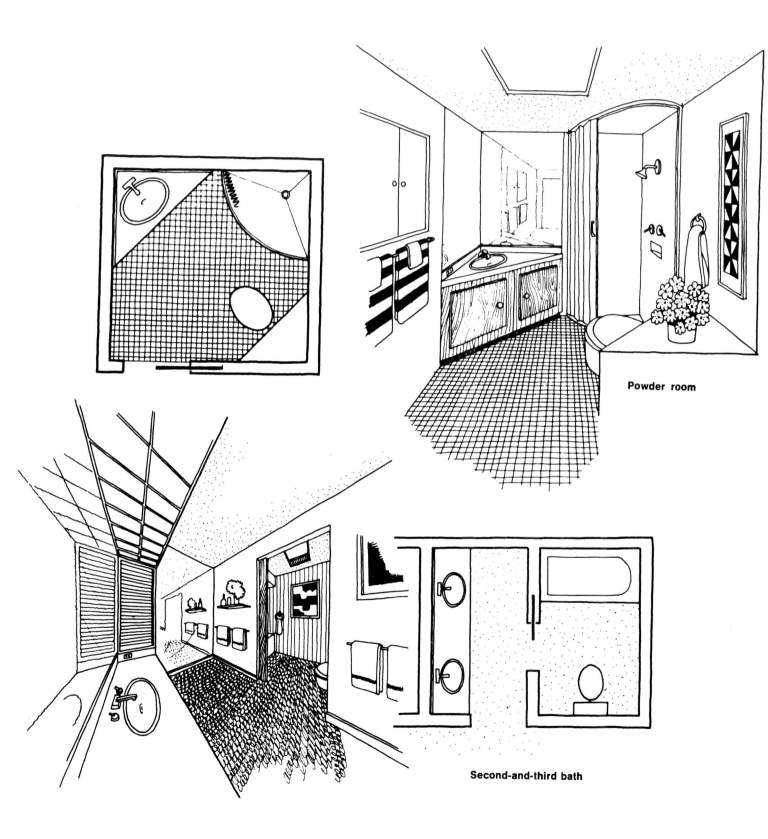

Powder room

Second-and-third bath

A small powder room can be turned into a full use bath with corner fixtures. Most fixture manufacturers have a scaled-down corner fixture line designed to make maximum use of those lost corners in a small room.

A corner sink and water-closet will make room for a corner shower — a perfect solution for a second bath off the mud room, family room or basement. To avoid space-stealing doors, install a sliding door or bi-folds. Lavish use of mirrors (especially a corner mirror over sink) will bounce image off of image for a much more spacious effect.

A second-and-third bath in one is the happy result of good compartmentalization. When a second bath has to serve two bedrooms (children's area), make it serve a double function.

The important thing to remember is isolate the bathtub and water closet, not the vanity. Again, if the space is small, use a sliding door between compartments. The first compartment housing the sinks should contain under-the-counter storage (wall-to-wall), end-wall medicine chests on each side, soffit to-splashboard mirror. Soffit lighting over the counter will give an even light distribution which will also make the area larger. Carpeting carried through from the bedroom into the first compartment will help it seem less like an isolated, small room and more like a part of the bedroom.

Inner Space: Divide and Conquer

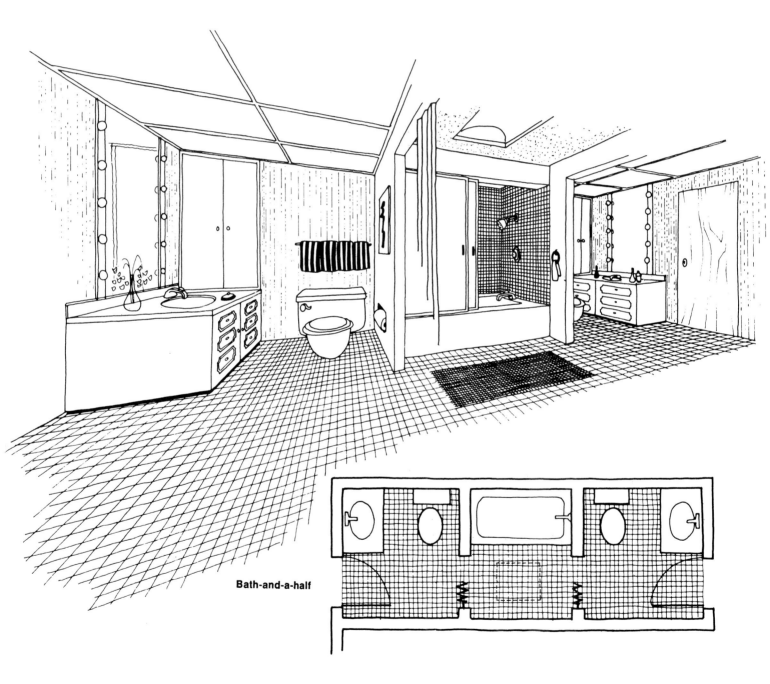

Bath-and-a-half

The bath-and-a-half is a variation on the double entry and compartmentalized bath. This three compartment bath is one of the most efficient ways to get full family use from one plumbing wall. The master suite bath (already compartmentalized) is extended to include another half-bath with separate entry. A tub compartment in the middle is made private with two bi-fold doors.

Each bath then borrows tub and shower facilities from the other. Privacy may be maintained in either end compartments. A skylight over the tub area and storage vanities in each end compartment makes this a real hard-working, three-way, second bath.

Compartmentalize with Confidence

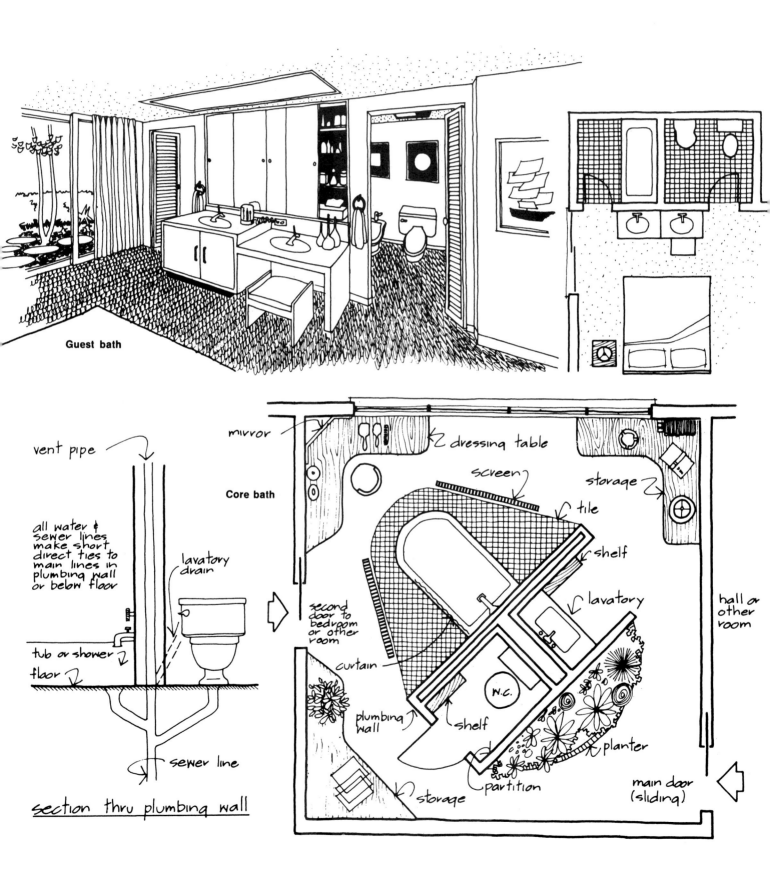

Guest bath

vent pipe

mirror

Core bath

all water & sewer lines make short direct ties to main lines in plumbing wall or below floor

lavatory drain

tub or shower

floor

sewer line

section thru plumbing wall

dressing table

screen

storage

tile

shelf

lavatory

hall or other room

second door to bedroom or other room

curtain

plumbing wall

shelf

N.C.

planter

partition

storage

main door (sliding)

The guest bath works best if put in the guest bedroom. A small area (opposite master bath plumbing wall perhaps) can hold the water closet and shower, and the vanity can become a handsome addition to the bedroom itself. Drop one basin, if there are two, to dressing table height. If there is only one, drop a portion of the counter. Rich wood-grained cabinets, sliding mirrored medicine chest and recessed ceiling lighting minimize the "bathroom" look, and rather than make the bedroom look smaller actually make it appear bigger — and a lot more luxurious.

A core bath is the perfect answer when a second bath is impossible. This sketch is a combination of some of the preceding techniques: double entry, compartmentalization, corner utilization, etc. It is actually a core system since the central plumbing wall holds all the fixtures.

Right angle compartmentalization and central placement makes it impossible to see all of this room at one glance or from one vantage point. Even though it requires a large space, it functions as three baths in one, eliminating the need for a second bath in another part of the house.

Carpeting, planters, corner storage and vanity makes this room functional; an attractive, highly merchandisable non-bathroom spa.

Buyers will not remember the house with only one bath, instead they will remember "that great 3-in-1 bathroom."

Family room

14 Storage: Housing for Possessions

Providing space for all kinds of personal possessions can go a long way in helping merchandise a model home or apartment. Any housing unit becomes much more livable when the spaces allotted to storage are carefully planned. This kind of well-designed storage is particularly effective where square footage is at a premium. Here are some ideas that will help your homes and apartments offer maximum utility and sales value for every square foot.

Family room storage is often entirely neglected, yet this is the one room in the house (aside from the kitchen) that draws to it more gadgetry and miscellany than any other. Since it is a heavily-used room, and since each member of the family has a claim on it, storage space should be carefully considered. Notice here how two factory-finished base cabinets (in the same style as the kitchen cabinets in the foreground) plus pre-finished shelving provide bonus space for books, magazines, records, hi-fi equipment and television. The base cabinet on the left is designed to hold games and entertaining equipment such as cocktail napkins, coasters, etc. This storage wall is far more than practical. It suggests to the prospect the various uses of the room — it virtually makes the room come alive.

Look Beyond the Linen Closet

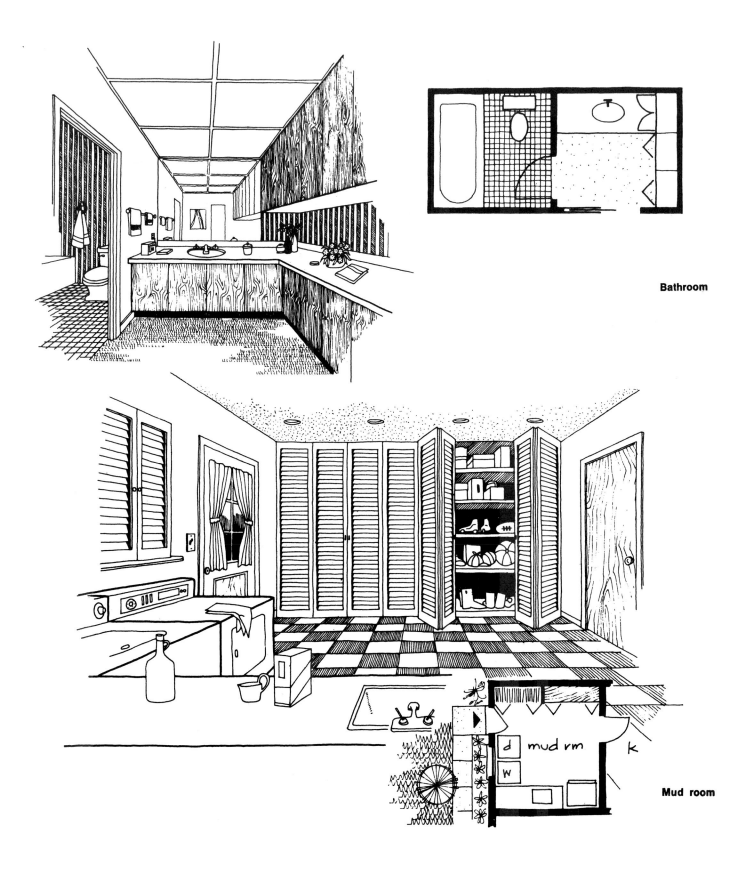

Bathroom

Mud room

Bathroom storage often stops with linen closets and an under-the-sink cabinet. But what about the many new appliances that are invading the bath? Hairdryers, electric hair curlers, "power" toothbrushes, etc., are too bulky for the medicine chest. Why not provide a "bath pantry" by extending the vanity cabinet around a corner? Overhead cabinets for towels and linens might take the place of the traditional linen closet and free some precious space for a larger second bedroom or more clothing storage for the master suite.

A mud room, however small, should provide space for golashes, raincoats, ice skates, sports equipment. A foot and a half of floor space covered with bi-folds provides real bonus storage where it's needed. This has particular appeal to buyers with young families.

Dull, Dark Corners
Become Super Storage Centers

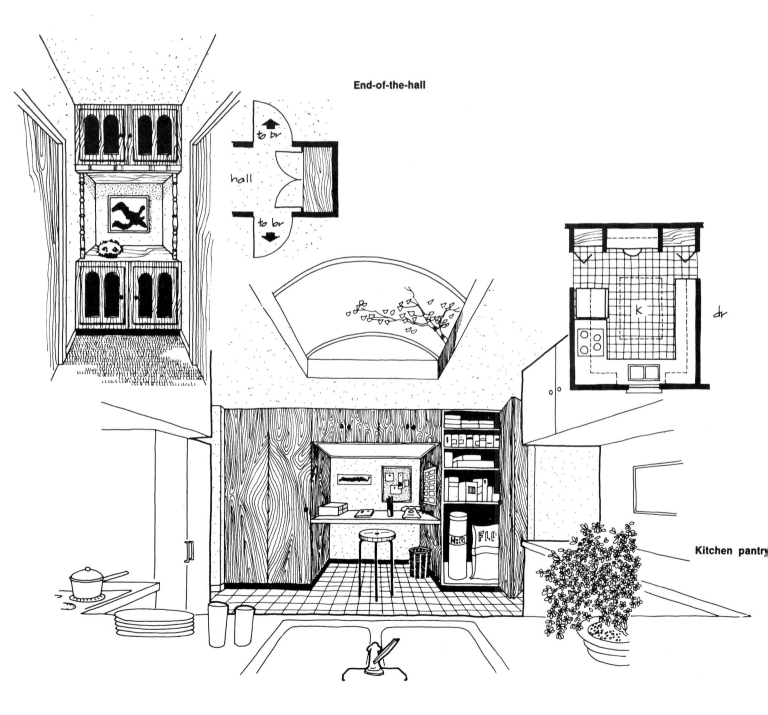

End-of-the-hall

to br

hall

to br

Kitchen pantry

End-of-the-hall or dead space is easily transformed into a useful storage area for linens, cleaning equipment, while at the same time making a bright focal point where before only a dark corner existed.

The kitchen pantry has made a comeback but in different clothing. Now, pantry cabinets made to match the rest of the kitchen cabinetry are needed to store the bulky items that are becoming more prevalent in the super markets. Large super-economy-sized boxes of soap or dog food don't fit in the ordinary base cabinets.

Another pantry cabinet, with interior shelving partially removed, houses brooms, mops, vacuum cleaners and a variety of household cleaning equipment. And a home-office center between the two units completes this storage wall.

Overhead cabinets for cookbooks or little-used cooking utensils may or may not be used, if not, a soffit with some built-in lighting would serve to tie the two elements together.

This storage treatment is particularly useful when a garden kitchen plan (sliding casements and pass-through to patio over sink) replaces much-needed overhead storage.

Rich wood grain patterns, used floor-to-ceiling, create a paneled look guaranteed to make any kitchen something special.

Masterminding the Master Suite

Master suite

mbr

The master suite has become firmly established as a powerful merchandising tool. If well planned, it can quickly convey a luxurious tone to the whole home or apartment. At its best, it is a masterful blend of storage, convenience and privacy. It is comfortable and intimate, holding the owner's or renter's most personal possessions.

This is why smart builders have compartmentalized the bath, stolen space from the bedroom proper and added a transitional dressing area between the two. The result of this shuffling of space is usually better storage facilities.

While walk-in closets are fine, they often represent more cubic space than usable space. It would be better to give some of that valuable space back to the bedroom, provide wardrobe closets with bi-folds, and auxiliary storage with base and overhead cabinets. The cabinets allow for specialized and organized storage of all foldable and bulky items plus two bonus advantages: one, they help furnish the room (especially good for apartments), and two, they release otherwise enclosed storage space to the room, helping to make it look bigger.

Arranged as they are in this sketch, they also act as a visual transition from bedroom to dressing area.

Closet Hardware Helps You Organize, Dramatize

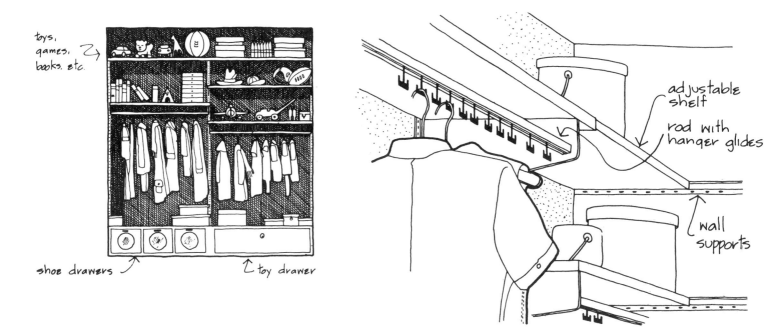

toys, games, books, etc.

shoe drawers

toy drawer

adjustable shelf

rod with hanger glides

wall supports

Closet organization

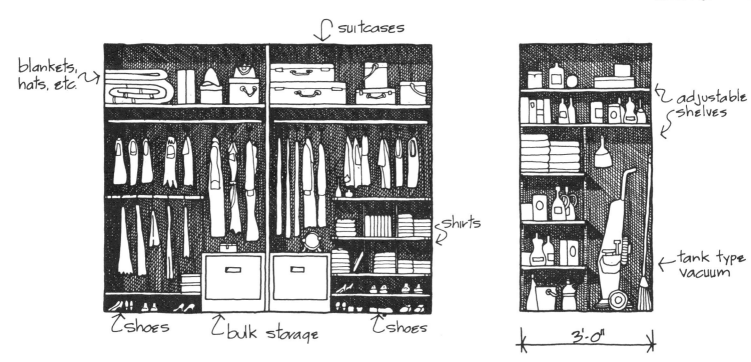

suitcases

blankets, hats, etc.

shirts

shoes

bulk storage

shoes

adjustable shelves

tank type vacuum

3'-0"

Closet organization (in models) can do much to solve one of the most common buyer or tenant complaints: "not enough storage space." A little forethought and small expense can transform an otherwise inadequate-looking closet into a super-useful storage center.

There are many products on the market designed to help you organize this space: expandable shelf-and-pole systems and a host of closet organizers complete with adjustable shelves, bins, sliding drawers, etc. Use them in your models and fill them with household items to dramatically merchandise the potential efficiency of storage space provided.

Free Standing Wall Works Well

Open plan design

Open-plan design and the current trend toward more and more glass often present a problem. Where does storage space fit in? Many of the walls where cabinets could be hung have been replaced with glass; interior partitions having been removed, the opportunities for closets are fewer.

The solution is often a free-standing storage unit, a storage island, or divider. In this kitchen-dining room plan, scant kitchen storage is supplemented with a large two-sided double-access storage center. Dishes, glassware, silverware, table linens and accessories may be removed from either the dining room side or the kitchen side.

A central pass-through functions as a serving bar, food preparation center and clean-up station. The storage center itself(when pass-through is closed) acts as a buffer between dining room and kitchen area without destroying the effect of the open plan. Sight lines move over and around it and don't interfere with the dramatic and spacious effect of the plan. When pass-through is open, the housewife can go about her chores without feeling removed from guests or family.

Providing effective storage is more important today than ever before. Space is at a premium, buyer demands in an affluent, possession-filled society are higher than ever. Lack of consideration in this one area can make an otherwise salable house or rentable apartment a near-miss.

Living room

15
Structural
Lighting

The most important showroom of all — the model home — is often placed before the customer with minimal thought given to lighting. Getting products into the model requires a great deal of ingenuity and planning. Why hide them? In today's highly competitive market-place, good lighting can make the difference. Following are examples of how both structural and fixture lighting will emphasize and glamorize the products, textures and colors in your model; how light can stretch space, dramatize height and create a buying mood.

The living room at the left illustrates three basic types of structural lighting: wall wash from recessed, eyeball fixtures; ceiling wash from cove lighting; and floor wash from under-the-built-in lighting. Both fluorescent and incandescent light combine to give the room a natural, outdoor-lighting effect. The swivel fixtures are ideal for giving textural emphasis to the fireplace wall and cost the smallest fraction of the wall itself. Space them 18″ apart and about 8″ to 16″ from the wall.

Cove lighting over the couch emphasizes the dramatic cathedral ceiling. Inexpensive fluorescent fixtures are appropriate since the light source is completely hidden. Make certain that this type of lighting is always at least 12″ away from ceiling. The more space the better.

A great space stretcher is the floor wash. Legless, built-in furniture (here a couch, but could be a vanity in master suite) exposes more floor space. A light under the built-in brings wasted square footage into the room. Here again, use fluorescent fixtures.

Illuminating for Luxury Living

RENDERINGS: ROGER JADOWN

Dining room

Bedroom

Today, formal dining rooms are in great demand, but it isn't always possible to provide them. In less expensive homes, where space is at a premium, it is usually better to use an open plan rather than chop whatever space is available for living into small cubes.

This doesn't mean, however, that you cannot create the effect of a formal dining room. Do it with lighting. A recessed ceiling spot — in this case a framing projector — or a dimmer frames the table with light making it a focal point. Framing projectors have a lens and shutter to concentrate light. If the lighting in the rest of the room is flexible (on dimmers) the dining area can take on all the importance and elegance of a formal dining room by just changing the lighting emphasis when dining.

After dinner, the table can be plunged into obscurity by switching the lighting emphasis back into the living room. Some low-voltage spots have been used in this sketch (attached to beams) to highlight paintings. These, along with a downspot on the plant, keep the walls of the area visual, thus maintaining a sense of space without emphasizing the clutter on the table.

Bedroom lighting is often the most neglected. A center ceiling dish fixture provides a bland, uninteresting light, good only for general illumination. Instead, a recessed ceiling wall washer or directional fixture can shed dramatic light on louvered closet doors, as well as shed light on the inside of the closet when doors are open. No fixture in the closet is necessary.

The overhead dish fixture can be replaced with bracket lighting. This useful type of structural lighting is easily accomplished. A wall mounted fluorescent fixture is covered with a simple wooden cornice (6″ deep). Lighting fixture should be at least 3″ away from wall for even distribution of light.

Cornice should be 2″ from fixture. For over-the-bed lighting place fixture 52″ from floor. Use one 30 or 40 watt lamp. Soffit lighting over work areas — in this case a study carrel — illuminates horizontal surfaces best. Use fluorescent fixtures with reflectors, paint inside of soffit flat black and cover with plastic or glass diffuser.

Stretch Space, Dramatize Height, Accent Features

Family room

Hallway

Today's family room has very special requirements. Because it is such a versatile room, handling so many of the family's activities, it should be well illuminated. But mere general illumination, without spots of dramatic lighting, can be dull. Try beam lighting, instead of just the usual box beams, install fluorescent fixtures in open boxes and cover with plastic diffuser.

Result is dramatic and practical. Lighted beams emphasize the cathedral ceiling and overhead space, and, at the same time, spread light evenly throughout the room. Drama can be added with a framing projector (recessed ceiling) on a picture, and low hung pendant lighting fixtures over a planter.

Bracket lighting washes the brick fireplace wall accenting the strong texture.

Hallways can be a serious problem. While taking up a considerable amount of floor space, they never seem to add to the livability of a home. Light can solve the problem. Luminescent wall panels (fluorescents placed between the studs and covered with a translucent material instead of wall board) can make the area glow with light and come alive. Functionally, of course, it ends the dark corridor look, but the psychological benefits are even greater. Dead floor space becomes alive . . . an extension of the active area of the home.

Special Effects for Special Spots

Flexible lighting

Bathroom

Pantries

Flexible lighting systems are now available from many manufacturers. While not considered structural because they are applied, they do everything that structural lighting can do. They illuminate a cathedral ceiling, wall wash, accent plants or pictures and produce down-light for specific activities (such as ping-pong in this sketch).

Light canisters are clipped on an electrified track, wherever they are needed (tracks come in three and four foot modules) and can be swiveled and tilted to serve any lighting need. Lamps are deeply recessed in canisters to hide light source as much as possible and eliminate glare.

Bathroom lighting is always important. Here three different light sources provide much more than utilitarian light.

A recessed down spot (1) in the shower area glances off tile wall and produces an almost theatrical effect when other lighting is subdued (on dimmer or turned off). Soffit lighting (2) over the vanity produces a good even light.

Same effect can be achieved with cornice light if economy prevents plastering in a soffit. While these two light sources are all that may be necessary for proper illumination, lighting experts have found that a direct source of light around the mirror (3) is required if the lady of the house is to feel "properly lighted for make-up". Many manufacturers produce highly interesting and decorative strip lighting for this purpose.

Now that pantries are back cabinet manufacturers are lavishing a great deal of attention on them. Handsome wood grains and opulent hardware can be dramatized to great effect with two or three recessed ceiling swivels. Just as with the louvered door closet on the preceding spread, these lights serve a dual purpose: they sell the rich cabinetry, and illuminate the interior.

Add Flexibility, Luxury, Security

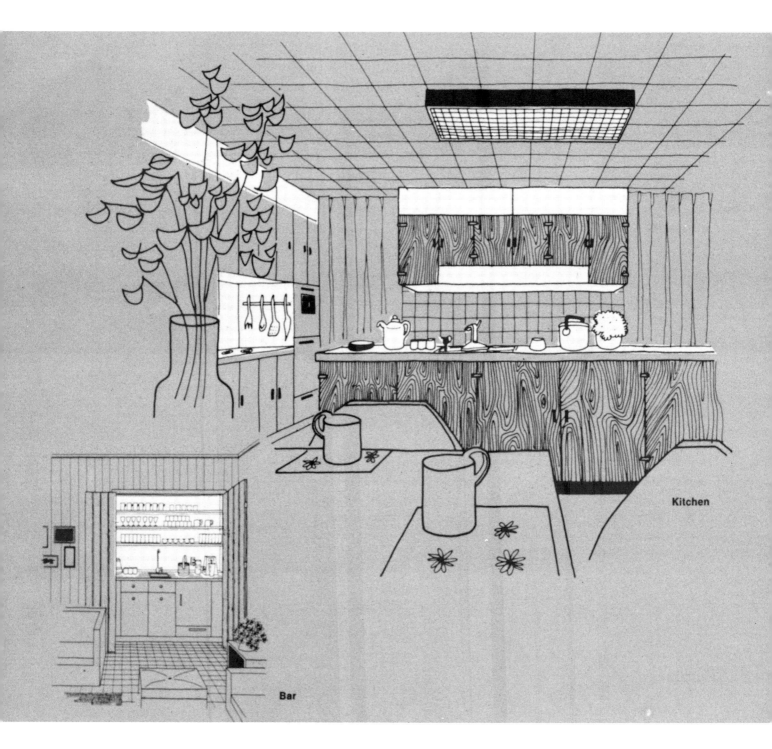

Kitchen

Bar

Kitchens have often been heralded as the most important room in the house. It is amazing how so much money can be spent on them without any thought to properly lighting this product-packed room. Appliances, cabinets, flooring, wall coverings should be emphatically displayed.

And since the kitchen is now so much a part of the family room (or living area in apartments), it should not be simply utilitarian but handsome. This can only be achieved with built-in flexible lighting.

Under-the-counter light is essential for food preparation, but can be turned off while serving. Soffit lighting over the cabinets can produce a floating effect that greatly expands a small kitchen. General illumination from luminescent ceilings or ceiling fixtures combine well with specific work light, but also can be turned off or dimmed for a more living room look.

Pendant fixtures or downspots over a breakfast bar produce entirely different effects. Use the pendant fixtures if a divider is needed; down spots if breakfast bar is in the kitchen proper and not the family room.

Bars are becoming more and more popular in the family room. Whether a de luxe wet-sink bar with under-the-counter refrigerator such as the one here, or simply a storage space for glasses and bottles with a work surface, light can make it seem very important. Simply have the counter top cut three inches narrower than usual and in the open space between wall and counter, drop a fluorescent fixture 2″ below counter level. Cover (at counter level) with transluscent glass.

The resulting up light washes back wall and diffuses through glass shelves and glassware. Balance with another fluorescent fixture mounted in the ceiling for downlight (or several incandescent recessed fixtures if door opening goes to ceiling).

Light Up the Exterior

Outdoor lighting

Outdoor lighting does the same thing that indoor lighting does: it merchandises the textures and materials of the model. Soffit lighting whether recessed spots or exposed canisters, glances against brick or rough-sawn sliding emphasizing the texture and color.

Entry lighting is best achieved with wall fixtures augmented by hidden spots. Walkway lighting and landscape lighting make even a modest sized home seem much larger.

The visual impact of the home is greatly extended by including all of the grounds with low voltage spots. Trees are best lighted with deep-recessed up-light canisters (eliminates the possibility of glare). Walkways, shrubs and flower beds come alive at night with low-voltage mushroom fixtures.

Patios, decks should be lighted with the same care as the interior — especially since today's smaller homes depend so much on outdoor living space to extend the floor plan. Light not only makes these areas usable at night, but greatly adds to the sense of interior dimension.

Single family as weil as multi-family units realize a significant bonus from outdoor lighting: security.

Take a tip from the top merchandisers. Plan ahead to bathe your product with mood-setting, space-making, exciting light. Don't hide everything you've done.

planning center

16
Custom Concepts

How to give a tailored look to merchant housing

Custom homes have traditionally set the trends in housing. And smart merchant builders have traditionally kept an eye on them for adaptable ideas which would help stamp their models with a little character of their own. The pages of this chapter offer a collection of "custom concepts," aimed at making a house more interesting, more memorable, therefore more salable.

Bold approach to planning center

Home planning centers are not unusual, even in less expensive homes. But too often they are approached too timidly and fail to make much of an impact on the customer. This is doubly regrettable since a well-designed planning center may actually cut cabinet costs. Instead of a solid wall of cabinets, use some matched shelving (supplied by almost all cabinet manufacturers) with two 24" base cabinets and the required number of 12" deep overhead cabinets to fill the wall. Telephone, intercom and electrical outlets for TV and lighting supply the necessary touches for a really high-impact custom kitchen.

Little Touches, Big Results

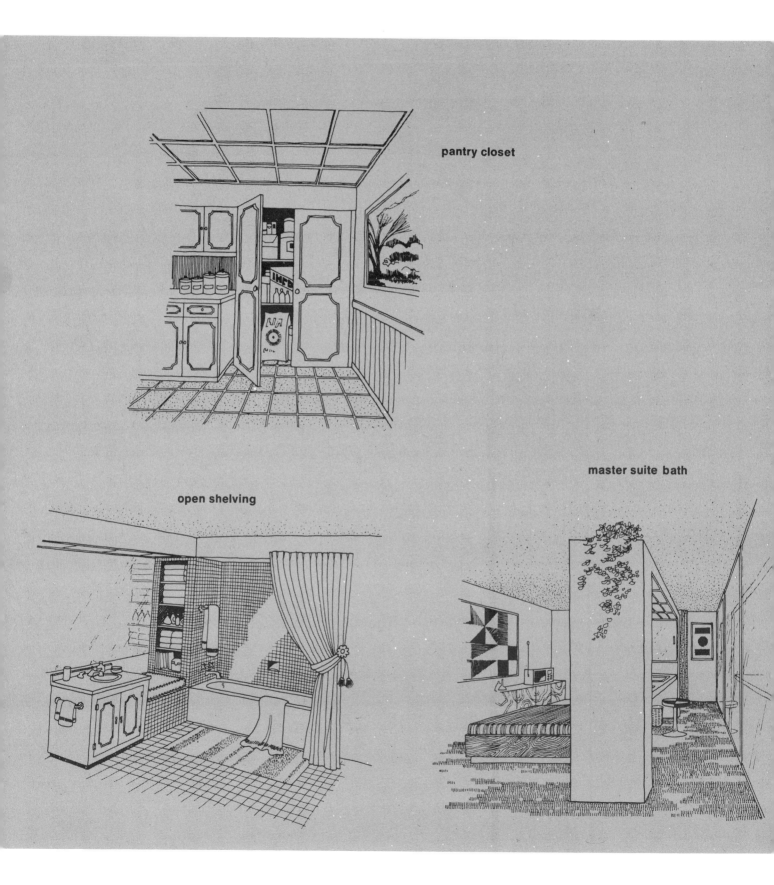

pantry closet

master suite bath

open shelving

Use cabinet moldings to tie in pantry closet

Pantries (upper left) have made a big comeback in the last few years. Cabinet manufacturers have recognized the need for bulk storage and provide a variety of solutions to the problem. Where an actual closet-type pantry is possible, apply moldings on doors to match the rest of the cabinetry in kitchen.

Design bathroom to fit master suite

Baths, second only to kitchens, grab the buyer's attention. By stealing space from what might have been a full bathroom and dressing area and making it a part of the bedroom itself, it is possible to build a floating partition to house the double vanity as well as provide a headboard wall for the king-size bed.

Add something special with open shelving

Open, recessed shelving can make a more conventional bathroom something special. Towel storage, usually relegated to a hall linen closet, becomes an added and almost focal feature of this small bath (lower left). A cushioned seating area next to tub and vanity can be a "memory point" with the housewife. Tile is pulled around the corner and across seating area and vanity to the tub-shower.

Simple Cabinet Treatments
Customize Central Living Areas

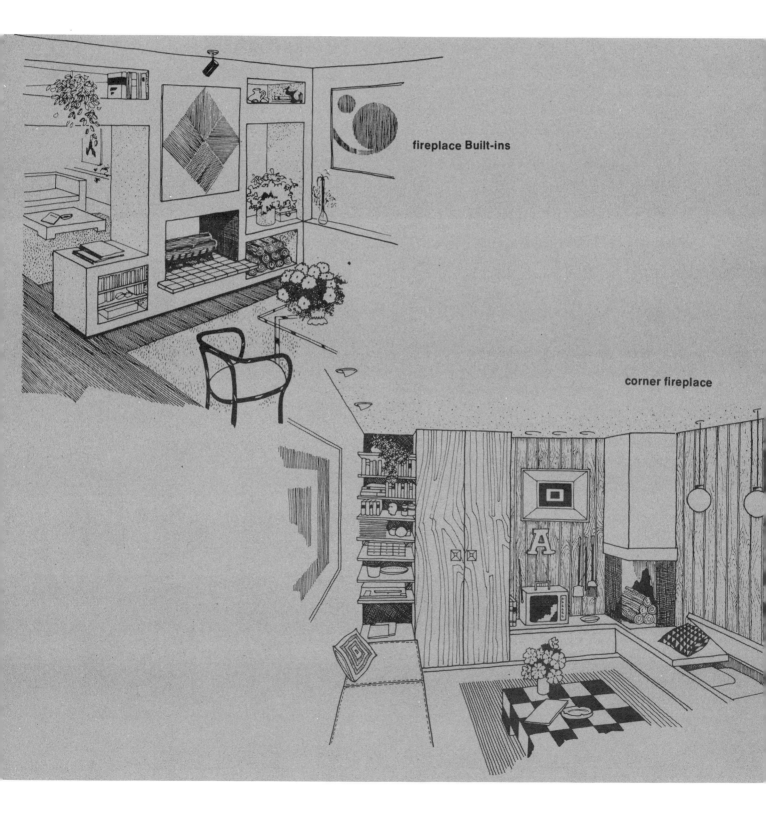

fireplace Built-ins

corner fireplace

Built-ins turn new attention to fireplace

A fireplace is always a plus in selling a house. But why not make it really important rather than just "there." This prefab fireplace (illustrated at left) is made to work triply hard. It serves both living and dining room, creates a divider wall, and supplies storage for logs, hi-fi and books. Compared to the initial expense of installing the fireplace, the additional framing and plasterboard is negligible.

A corner fireplace becomes focal point

When the family room gets the fireplace, extend its function with simple built-in seat-shelving 12 in. from the floor, as suggested in this corner arrangement. By hinging the top of the boxes, seating can double for game storage. Cedar plywood lining turns it into out-of-season clothing storage. But the real merchandising benefit lies in the added emphasis it gives to the corner fireplace.

Build in Richness with Cabinets, Shelves

dining room

bookcase

Give the dining room a sense of importance

Dining rooms are often just plain boxes depending almost wholly on a chandelier to define its use. With the growth of interest in formal dining, this neglected room should receive more attention. Here, applied moldings under a simple wainscoting make it read "dining room" immediately. Added customizing in more expensive homes can be achieved with factory finished cabinets. Two cabinets mounted sideways facing each other on opposite end walls tied together with a shelf covered with plastic laminate (use one of the more formal new leather textures), results in a bonus sideboard plus silver and china storage. If using unique moldings in room, buy flush cabinets and apply matching moldings to them.

Make an impression with a bookcase

Bookcases may be a minor item, but they make quite an impression in an otherwise plain living room. This is a particularly useful customizing feature when there is no fireplace or other unusual architectural feature in the living room. Placed on each side of a window the window itself takes on more architectural importance and depth.

Built-ins That Make a Bedroom More Than a Place to Sleep

window seat

closet vanity

Window seat offers sentimental charm

The charm of a window seat, whether in a bay or a single dormer window, evokes sentimental reaction from a buyer, particularly in a bedroom where a sense of privacy or quiet repose is desired. It is a uniquely effective custom device in smaller homes where space is at a premium. The smallest master bedroom can appear larger and can be made to accommodate a "lounging area" with the mere addition of a few cushions and a small-scaled coffee table.

Small vanity adds to closet wall

A between-the-closet vanity is another way to stretch space in a small master suite as well as add a custom touch. Sliding mirrored doors on Mr. and Mrs. Closets are divided by a simple shelf vanity. Another mirror behind the shelf adds surprisingly more dimension to the room, since the wall mirror and closet door mirrors are on different planes, creating different dimensional reflections. Glass shelves and a ceiling soffit light add to the total effect.

Motel Ideas That Work at Home

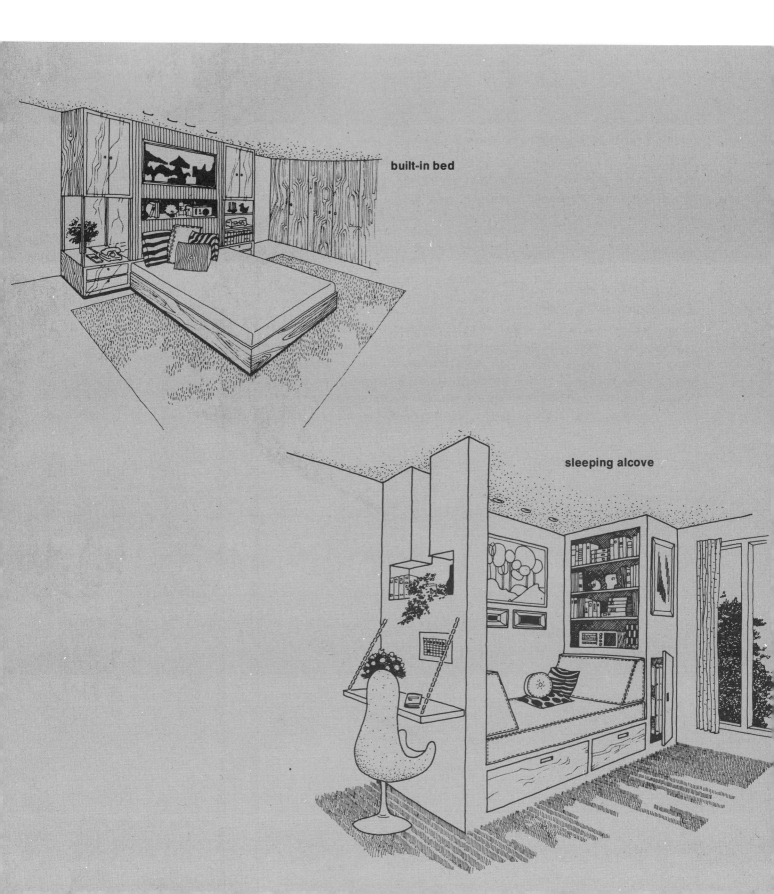

built-in bed

sleeping alcove

Borrow from motels with built-in bed

Built-in beds are becoming more and more popular, especially in second home condominiums and rentals. Chalk up the interest to hotel and motel design. Handsome plywood paneling or vertical strips of flooring form a headboard, and a simple frame and slats form the bed. For more elaborate version, add end table, shelving or, as pictured here, combination overhead storage units and night stands.

A sleeping alcove for multi-purpose use

Second bedrooms often have to double in brass as guest rooms or dens. Built-in bed, with or without storage below, can answer many of the needs of a multi-purpose room. A shelf-desk at one end of the sleeping alcove becomes a study carrel if a child's room, a writing desk if a den. Depending upon how elaborate the price tag, bookshelves and additional storage can be built in.